insight text guide

Anica Boulanger-Mashberg

Mabo

Dir. Rachel Perkins

First published in 2013, reprinted in 2014, 2017.

Insight Publications Pty Ltd
3/350 Charman Road
Cheltenham VIC 3192
Australia
Tel: +61 3 8571 4950
Fax: +61 3 8571 0257
Email: books@insightpublications.com.au

www.insightpublications.com.au

National Library of Australia Cataloguing-in-Publication entry:
Boulanger-Mashberg, Anica, author.
Rachel Perkins' Mabo / Anica Boulanger-Mashberg.
9781922243263 (paperback)
Insight text guide.
Includes bibliographical references.
For secondary school age.
Perkins, Rachel–Criticism and interpretation.
Mabo (Motion picture)
791.4372

Cover design: The Modern Art Production Group

Printed in Australia

contents

CHARACTER MAP

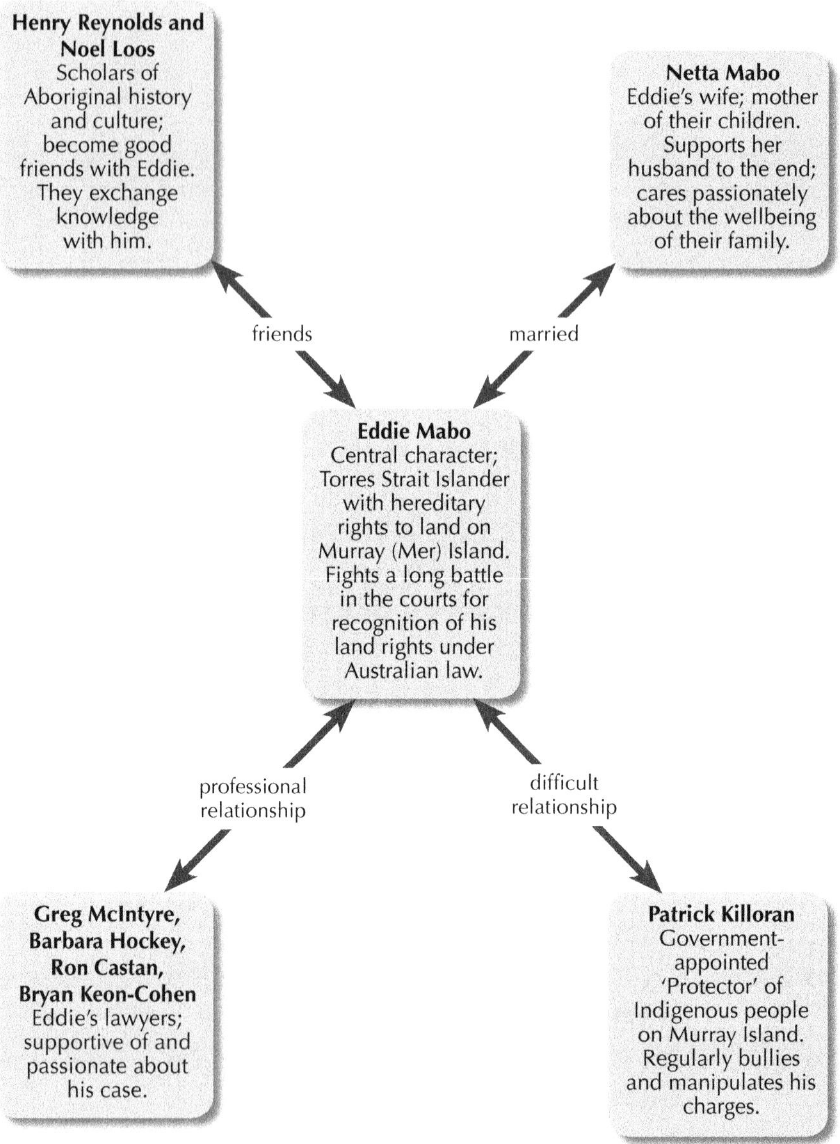

Aboriginal and Torres Strait Islander readers are respectfully advised that this guide contains names of deceased people.

OVERVIEW

About the filmmakers

Script

The screenplay for *Mabo* (2012) is by Sue Smith, an award-winning writer who has made an important contribution to Australian television over her long career. She has also written for film and stage, but is best known for her television writing, which includes series and miniseries such as *Brides of Christ* (1991), about young women's lives in a convent; *Bastard Boys* (2007), about the battles between wharf workers' unions and industry and government bodies in 1998; and several episodes of *RAN* (*Remote Area Nurse*) (2006), set in the Torres Strait and focusing on the experiences of Torres Strait Islanders and Indigenous Australians. She has a particular interest in Australian stories, and many of her works are about aspects of Australian life – historical and contemporary, rural and urban, Indigenous and non-Indigenous.

For *Mabo*, Smith received an AWGIE (Australian Writers' Guild award) and won the category for television scripts in the Queensland Literary Awards.

Direction

Mabo is directed by Rachel Perkins, whose career has encompassed directing, writing and producing for film and television. She has won awards as both a writer and a director, and has been actively involved in the Australian film industry through roles on the Screen Australia board and in the Australian Film Commission. She also contributes to the industry through her participation in film festivals and with her production company, Blackfella Films (producers of *Mabo*).

Perkins has played a significant role in sourcing, developing and communicating narratives of Indigenous experience. Some of her most successful works as a director include *Radiance* (1998), *One Night the Moon* (2001) and *Bran Nue Dae* (2010), all of which centre on issues faced by Indigenous Australians. She was also responsible for the documentary series *First Australians* (and the accompanying books, website and community outreach program), which explores Australian Indigenous history.

Perkins' heritage is with the Arrernte and Kalkadoon Indigenous nations in Central Australia and Queensland.

Other important contributors

Unlike novels, television scripts often involve a degree of collaboration, and Sue Smith had assistance from a number of people. For example, she spent time with Eddie Mabo's wife, ***Bonita Mabo***, during the research period. The telemovie also credits two cultural consultants: ***Gail Mabo*** (daughter of Eddie and Bonita) and ***Charles Passi*** (son of Dave Passi). Their role included contributing knowledge and expertise in a number of areas, finding performers and extras by drawing on their links with Indigenous communities, and even providing set dressings for the production.

As with any film or television production, many departments and individuals contribute, but the director is ultimately responsible for the final product. As such, it is acceptable to discuss the decisions and intentions of the director (just as we might discuss the decisions of an author of a novel), even when those decisions may well have been the responsibility of others – such as the director of photography (in this case, Andrew Commis).

Synopsis

Mabo tells the story of Murray Islander Koiki, or Eddie, Mabo, who made a significant contribution to Australian history through his involvement in a groundbreaking legal case in the late 1980s and early 1990s that paved the way for the introduction of native title legislation. Eddie was a passionate activist for Indigenous and Torres Strait Islander rights, and also raised ten children with his wife, Bonita (although not all those children are present in this adaptation of his story).

In this telemovie, we first meet Eddie as a young boy, walking the shoreline on Murray Island (or Mer Island, as it is referred to in the traditional Meriam language spoken in the area) with his adoptive father, Benny Mabo. Benny tells Eddie about his heritage, responsibilities, rights and connection to the island. This image and Benny's words recur regularly, as they influence Eddie's values, motivation, confidence, beliefs and actions throughout his life.

After being forced to leave the island at age nineteen in punishment for a crime of social misbehaviour, Eddie meets and marries Bonita (Netta), who becomes his strongest support, raising their children and standing by him. Eddie, a passionate man with a strong sense of justice, never simply accepts situations that are less than satisfactory, but works to better himself through self-education and maintains a commitment to his values. He is an active union member in his early working life, and soon turns his activism to Indigenous and Islander rights – a passion that Netta sometimes considers foolish in the face of the everyday challenges of feeding and raising their growing family.

When he discovers that he has no legal claim, under Australian law, to his island homeland, Eddie launches a land-rights claim that will dominate the rest of his life. The legal battle goes through many challenges, frequently running out of funds, winning and losing various stages and eventually concluding in a High Court case, which sets a historic precedent, finding in favour of Eddie and the native title. In its findings, the High Court decision destroys the previously accepted legal doctrine of 'terra nullius' – the notion of Australia as an empty land, belonging to no-one, prior to European settlement.

Sadly, Eddie does not live to celebrate the historic announcement, having lost his fight with cancer only months earlier.

Character summaries

Koiki 'Eddie' Mabo (born Edward Koiki Sambo)

A proud Murray Islander who has lived most of his life off the island, Eddie is the central character. Married to Netta and father of their ten children, he loves his family but is regularly preoccupied with 'black causes': fighting for Indigenous rights, and engaging in legal battles with the government for recognition of his ownership of land on Murray. Eddie works in a number of different jobs during his life, is headmaster of a community school for Indigenous children, works hard to educate himself and plans to one day return to his land to live.

Note: Although Eddie tells Netta his name is 'Koiki for real' (Chapter Two), in much of the press coverage at the time he was known as Eddie, and the majority of this story is about his interactions with a 'whitefella' Australia, so in this guide he is referred to as Eddie.

Bonita 'Netta' Mabo

Eddie's wife, Netta, stands by her husband throughout the many challenges posed by his court cases. She cares about their family above all else, although she does broadly agree with Eddie's political agenda. Netta is Indigenous, but not from Murray Island. She is loyal and loving but also strong, stubborn, resourceful and practical.

Benny Mabo

Benny is a largely absent character – we see him in several early scenes, and in flashbacks to Eddie's childhood. Benny was actually Eddie's uncle, and adopted him at an early age. Eddie has always associated his heritage with Benny and the Mabo family, rather than with his birth family. In this guide, unless specified, references to Eddie's 'father' are to Benny (not to Robert Sambo, Eddie's birth father).

Patrick Killoran

A non-Indigenous bureaucrat responsible (under the Aboriginal and Torres Strait Islander Protection Act) for the welfare of Islanders in Queensland. He frequently exerts his power by intimidating his charges.

Noel Loos and Henry Reynolds

Academics specialising in Aboriginal history, Loos and Reynolds exchange knowledge with Eddie, encourage his activism and become his friends.

Greg McIntyre and Barbara Hocking

These two lawyers from the Aboriginal and Torres Strait Islander Legal Service in Cairns initially take on Eddie's land-rights claim. Greg McIntyre eventually represents Eddie separately in the final High Court challenge.

Ron Castan and Bryan Keon-Cohen

Lawyers from Melbourne, these two men work on Eddie's land-rights claim and on the High Court case.

Davy

A friend of Eddie's who takes the railway medical in his place.

The Mabo children

Eddie and Netta's children are minor characters (they are rarely named, and their births often not even mentioned; the size of the family simply increases with time). Yet they are often present at key moments, and are the central focus of Netta's energies.

David Passi, Sam Passi and James Rice

Fellow plaintiffs (among others) in Eddie's original land-rights claim; David and James also return for the High Court case.

Margaret White

A lawyer and the opposing counsel in the land-rights (and later High Court) case.

Justice Moynihan

The Supreme Court judge presiding over Eddie's land-rights claim in Queensland.

BACKGROUND & CONTEXT

Production details

The Blackfella Films production, first broadcast by ABC Television in June 2012 (after a screening at the Sydney Film Festival earlier that month), marked the twenty-year anniversary of the historically significant Mabo decision. Director Rachel Perkins made the film with the support and assistance of many Mabo family members, including Eddie's wife, Bonita, and daughter Gail, and other members of the Murray Island community.

Despite the fact that the telemovie chronicles the life of a man whose achievements were remarkable, as well as depicting the lives of those closest to him, it does not glorify those it portrays. Rather, it offers a realistic insight into the life of Eddie Koiki Mabo: a man who was passionate and committed, but certainly not always easy. This is an honest, 'warts and all' portrait of Eddie that his family were happy to offer to the world.

Mabo was well received by the Indigenous community, and won Film of the Year, Male Actor of the Year (Jimi Bani) and Female Actor of the Year (Deborah Mailman) in the 2012 Deadlys – the National Aboriginal & Torres Strait Islander Music, Sport, Entertainment & Community Awards.

Geographical/social setting

Although the majority of *Mabo* takes place on mainland Australian soil – primarily in Queensland, where Eddie lived much of his life – its thematic heart is Eddie's home island, the land over which his legal claims were lodged. Murray Island is one of the Torres Strait islands that lie between Australia and Papua New Guinea, off the north-east coast of Far North Queensland. The traditional cultures on individual islands in the Torres Strait share some elements, but they also have many discrete laws, customs, languages and spiritual beliefs. Similarly, while Islander cultures share some things with mainland Indigenous Australian cultures, and Islanders are Indigenous peoples, Islanders should be considered distinct from mainland Indigenous peoples. Often the two groups are combined, however, for administrative, legal, historical and broad cultural purposes.

In 1879 the British annexed Murray Island, along with the majority of the Torres Strait Islands, to Queensland, and so they came under the jurisdiction of the Queensland government. In *Mabo*, it is this government which seeks to oppose Eddie's land-rights claim.

For further information on Murray Island and the Torres Strait region, see the links included under 'References'.

Australian race relations

As Richard Broome observes in his history of Aboriginal Australians, European settlement of Australia brought many challenges: 'the practices of colonialism narrowed and shaped the options of both Indigenous and settler Australians' (Broome 2009, pp.2–3). The state of race relations between Indigenous and non-Indigenous Australians at the time of Eddie's case is an important backdrop to the drama.

In the late 1950s and early 1960s – some of Eddie's formative years of early adulthood – non-Indigenous perceptions of Indigenous Australians tended to discrimination, judgement and racism (a belief in the superiority of one's own race and, therefore, the right to mistreat those of other races). Such views were formally endorsed by government policy, particularly in the conservative state of Queensland. The general belief at this time was that Indigenous and mixed-race Australians should be assimilated into the white Australian community, whether culturally – by replacing Indigenous cultural customs with non-Indigenous ones – or biologically, by a process called **miscegenation** (interbreeding with the intention of breeding out the race considered inferior). Many cultural, social and governmental practices accompanied this philosophy, from discrimination against individuals to the forced removal of Indigenous and mixed-race children from their homes and families, often with a supposed justification of offering them better lives with white families.

The notions of assimilation and an ideal of a 'White Australia' supported widely held beliefs that Indigenous Australians were not just different but also inferior, and in need of improvement so that they could live up to white Australian standards and move from a 'primitive' to a 'civilised' cultural existence. (Though assimilation policies were predominant at this time, many people still subscribed to earlier beliefs about segregation – keeping Indigenous people at a distance so as not to 'contaminate' the non-Indigenous population.)

In the 1960s, federal and state laws still treated Indigenous people differently from non-Indigenous people, regulating many areas of their lives, including the consumption of alcohol, the ability to vote, and even the right to marry who they chose. This was not an easy time to be an Aboriginal or Torres Strait Islander in Australia, as we see in some of the archival footage in *Mabo*, such as the interviews with individuals who describe how Indigenous people are refused service and only allowed to attend the cinema by entering through separate doors and sitting in a separate section (Chapter Four). In that same chapter, we hear Netta's experience of having to wait while all the white people were served before her. These experiences of discrimination represent the prevailing treatment facing Australians of Indigenous heritage in this era.

Yet the 1960s was also a period of great change, not only in Australia but also in other Western countries, such as the United States. Individuals were resisting authority and finding power in unionism and activism; they sought ways to make their voices heard in order to bring about change in their societies. Many Australians, Indigenous and non-Indigenous alike, were increasingly unhappy with the state of the race relations in the nation. An example of such allied activism was the formation, in the late 1950s, of Aboriginal Advancement Leagues – organisations of both Indigenous and non-Indigenous Australians whose goal was to improve the rights of Aboriginal Australians. These organisations first included all

Indigenous peoples collectively; then, from the mid-1960s, Torres Strait Islanders were considered as a separate Indigenous cultural group. In *Mabo,* the developments in activism are reflected when Eddie refers to the support he was offered by the Aboriginal Advancement League in Cairns to try to set up a union for waterside workers.

These bodies of support and advocacy (and their corresponding national body, the Federal Council for Aboriginal Advancement) began to have an impact on – or perhaps helped to reflect the change in – public opinion. In the 1967 referendum, an overwhelming majority of Australians voted to amend the constitution to include voting rights for Indigenous Australians, as well as their right to be recognised and legislated for at a federal level. Some years later, in 1975, the Whitlam government passed the Racial Discrimination Act, which was designed to protect Indigenous Australians against the sorts of unfair treatment they had received in the past. However, as Broome notes, the Act did 'not have criminal sanctions' and could do 'little to change attitudes' (Broome 2009, p.225). Thus, many Indigenous Australians still suffered (and continue to suffer) unfair discrimination, whether from their non-Indigenous neighbours in local shops, pubs or hotels (as we see in Eddie and Netta's experiences), or formally, in administrative treatment by individual state governments.

Government policy and public opinion slowly began to shift towards integration, and eventually 'equality', rather than assimilation, and states began to introduce legislation that covered land rights. Notably, this did not include Queensland, which, from the late 1960s to the late 1980s – under the leadership of then premier Joh Bjelke-Petersen – maintained a steadfastly conservative approach to race relations. The Queensland government continued to sanction many forms of discrimination, with much more stringent restrictions on Indigenous people's lives than in other states.

Even moves towards 'equality', however, did not always lead to 'fair' treatment for those who had been dispossessed of land by colonial settlement. For example, in the views of some people, since non-Indigenous Australians could not claim any special land rights, it would be unfair – indeed, *unequal* – for Indigenous people to have this opportunity. These beliefs, along with fears that native title would hinder development (especially in areas such as agriculture and mining) and damage Australia's financial and social position, led to the kinds of resistance we see in *Mabo* towards Indigenous land claims.

It is against this background of historical discrimination, increasing community awareness and activism, and conservative state government policy that *Mabo* is set.

Legal context

Although large sections of *Mabo* take place in the courtroom or focus on discussions of the cases, little specific legal knowledge is needed to follow the action. The script is written for a popular audience who, equipped with a basic understanding of terms such as plaintiff, brief and evidence, will have sufficient contextual knowledge to comprehend the events and the narrative.

GENRE, STRUCTURE & LANGUAGE

Genre

Mabo fits into several genres, including docudrama, courtroom drama, historical drama and biopic. Of these, the one which probably contributes most to an interpretation of the narrative is biopic. While the story is about a historical legal battle with far-reaching social and cultural impacts, primarily it is the tale of one man's life: of his political battles, his family and his love of his ancestral land.

Docudrama: fact and fiction

This production prioritised veracity and accuracy, as evidenced by Gail Mabo's involvement as cultural consultant. Many of the filming locations were the places where the real events occurred, and the set dressings (including family photographs and Eddie's sketches of Murray Island) were the authentic objects belonging to the Mabo family. However, the production is a *dramatic reconstruction* and not a *documentary* of this significant Australian's life and work.

It is important to note that although Eddie Mabo and his legal battles were the inspiration and central reference point for this production, the telemovie is still a dramatisation of the events and relationships that constitute this history. When discussing the narrative, you should aim to keep the factual, historical story of Mabo separate from the story told in this production. For example, if you research the background, you may discover personal or legal details about Eddie or his case which are not in the telemovie but which help you to contextualise and understand the story. However, they may not be relevant to discuss in essays if they are not part of the narrative that Sue Smith and Rachel Perkins have chosen to convey.

Q How does the story told in *Mabo* differ from a documentary of Eddie Mabo's life?

Structure

Time passes very swiftly in *Mabo* – the timeframe covered in less than two hours is approximately thirty-six years – and scenes tend to be short and episodic. Often, major life events are represented with a single scene or even a shot, with minimal dialogue. An example is Eddie and Netta's wedding, of which we only see a moment: their joyous departure afterwards. This technique allows the screenplay to encompass the lifetime of its central character, focusing on key moments and events.

Occasionally the production uses simple subtitles when shifting time or place (such as 'Townsville, 1967'), but otherwise the audience is expected to deduce from context where and when the scene is occurring. Because the style is a fairly straightforward example of the docudrama genre (the medium of television is not employed to manipulate the reality of the situation, but to tell the story in a realistic way), this is usually easy: for example, when we see the Mabos' first child, we know immediately that several years have passed since their wedding. Simple strategies such as this, and the ageing of the characters (especially as indicated by hair colour and style), indicate the passing of time.

The telemovie frequently makes use of imagery, symbolism and cinematic techniques – such as flashbacks or slow motion – to help tell the story efficiently. For example, when the High Court case results are announced towards the end of the narrative, Netta and her son joyfully embrace the non-Indigenous couple who have been listening to the radio news bulletin with them. This image succinctly tells us that the result of the case offers hope for the future of Australian race relations.

With the exception of several flashbacks, the progression of time in the narrative is unidirectional: it doesn't move backwards and forwards in Eddie's life. Nor is the story told from multiple perspectives or with the inclusion of scenes from far outside the chronological boundaries of Eddie's lifespan (apart from the final flashback). This encourages us to relate more directly to Eddie and his family, rather than to view Eddie's story as omnipresent or omnipotent outsiders.

Key point

Mabo uses narrative viewpoint to help guide our response to the story. Because as viewers our knowledge and experience of the events is most closely aligned with Eddie's knowledge and experience, we are likely to empathise strongly with *his* views and desires – rather than, for example, with the views and desires of other characters such as the members of the legal teams.

Language

There are a number of ways in which language contributes to *Mabo*. Two important areas to consider are the use of cinematic techniques as the 'language' with which the story is told, and the various forms of spoken language used by different characters.

Vocabulary

The majority of the dialogue in *Mabo* is in English, although on occasion Eddie or other characters speak in their traditional language. An example is the early scene with Eddie and Benny – their dialogue is spoken in Meriam, with English subtitles. This approach allows for both understanding and naturalism; the characters speak in their own language, but viewers who do not understand this language have an insight into what is being said.

There are also times when individual Meriam or Torres Strait Creole words such as 'kai kai' (meaning either 'food' or 'eat') make their way into the daily English of the characters. These are not subtitled, as their meaning is clear from context. Other features of the vocabulary used by the central characters include:

- informal speech patterns, such as dropping the letter 'g' from words ending in 'ing', or using words like 'gonna'
- colloquial or slang terms such as 'blackfella', 'whitefella', 'lock-up' or 'drink' (as a noun, meaning alcohol).

Such choices of vocabulary serve to develop both individual character – including background and attitude – and also broader settings, such as socioeconomic status.

Language style can provide viewers with a great deal of information about characters' experiences and personalities. For example, Eddie's vocabulary is often similar to that of the other Indigenous characters (he uses slang and informal speech patterns such as dropping the final 'g' in words), but it is sometimes markedly different. One instance is in Chapter Seven, when he defines the word 'impecunious', subverting his lawyer's expectation that this word would be beyond his knowledge. We see Eddie reading a dictionary during his early days in Queensland and discover that his reputation for self-education is widely recognised by the other characters. In his use of sophisticated vocabulary, then, an important feature of his character is illustrated.

Cinematic language

Unlike written texts, films and telemovies have at their disposal many layers of communication: verbal, visual and aural. Within these forms, nuance can also be created by filming and editing techniques, such as the timing or juxtaposition of shots. These elements function in much the same way as the use of language in a written text – for example, the juxtaposition of events in successive shots can create pacing and rhythms that influence audiences in the same way as the placement of information in successive chapters in a novel might influence readers.

An early moment between Eddie and Netta is an example of how cinematic techniques contribute to the narrative. When Eddie calls to Netta and their eyes meet, there is a moment of partial slow motion as she walks away from him, accompanied by the soundtrack and a glowing, warm afternoon light. These choices help us to understand the significance of the moment, and, although there is no dialogue involved, the message conveyed is very clear. Here, the 'language' of film functions just as written language functions in a print text: to focus our attention on specific details that inform us about the importance of characters, relationships and events.

Q Focus on a character other than Eddie. What does their vocabulary usage tell you about their background and personality?

Q What are some of the other cinematic techniques used in *Mabo* (such as lighting, soundtrack or cinematography)? How do they contribute to our understanding of the story?

SCENE-BY-SCENE ANALYSIS

Note: Chapter divisions used here are those provided by the DVD menu.

Chapter One (00:00)

Summary: *Archival news footage and a series of flashbacks, including the young Eddie with Benny, Eddie participating in a ceremonial dance and Eddie watching the women during church-choir practice.*

The telemovie opens with archival news footage relating to the Mabo case: snippets of reports and opinions about what was happening in the native title case. These snippets set a stylistic pattern for the narrative: the telemovie is made up of mostly short shots and scenes, allowing it to compress the whole of Eddie's life into less than two hours. Events frequently follow on from each other very quickly (such as in Chapter Two, when Eddie's marriage is immediately followed by a scene featuring his first child), and there is a sense of 'snapshot' storytelling: dialogue is often minimal, and close-ups or wordless images form rich sources of information.

The news footage is closely followed by **establishing shots** of Murray Island (**long shots** of the landscape and coastline from above, and **medium shots** of rainforest landscapes), and images of Eddie walking at the water's edge with his father. Benny tells him of their heritage and connection to the land. This scene recurs regularly through the film, as Eddie's thoughts return to the island and to his father. Within the first moments of the film, then, we know that the central issues will be the court case, the land on Murray Island and familial relationships.

The **montage** of flashbacks to Eddie's past is extended to include an adult Eddie in different settings: participating in a ceremonial dance and singing in a church choir (and finding himself distracted by the women in the choir). The film then settles into its first proper scene: Eddie in the island court in 1956 (the first of many court scenes for Eddie), on charges of behaving inappropriately with a member of the opposite sex. The court determines that he should be punished with a twelve-month exile to the mainland, where Benny worries that Eddie, like other young men who leave the island, will 'forget everything' about his heritage, family and island life.

We next meet Patrick Killoran, the Protector, who offers Eddie an alternative to the banishment: working for the rubbish-collection service. But Eddie refuses to work 'as a slave' and instead leaves (despite Killoran's efforts to discourage him) for western Queensland, to work on the railways, where he can earn some money.

Key point

This is the first time that we see Eddie's stubborn pride: he is not prepared to settle for what the world offers him when he thinks it is less than acceptable, instead seeking out alternatives and improving his prospects.

One of the last things we learn of in this chapter is Eddie's union involvement. He attends a meeting, and willingly steps up to the challenge of attracting more Islanders to the cause; he writes home to his father (in a letter that we hear in **voice-over**) describing how he is recruiting Islanders to the union so that they can all be represented. Union membership and union politics will continue to be important issues for Eddie in his working life.

Key vocabulary

Protector: a non-Indigenous administrator responsible for the protection of Indigenous people under the Aboriginal and Torres Strait Islander Protection Act. 'Protection' in this context had very different meanings for Indigenous and non-Indigenous people: what was seen as protective by the government was not always welcome for those covered by the Act.

Q What are the most important aspects of Eddie's character that we learn from this chapter?

Chapter Two (7:36)

Summary: *Eddie is denied service at a pub; he first meets Netta and embarrasses her by bringing alcohol into her cousin's wedding; he writes to her to apologise.*

This chapter opens with the first evidence of the discrimination Eddie and other Aboriginal and Torres Strait Islanders of the time were experiencing. When Eddie enters a pub with his colleagues, instead of being served with them, he is sent out the back to have his drink. His non-Indigenous mates barely bat an eyelid (though one casually says to the barman that it seems a 'bit rough'): this was the norm at the time. Eddie doesn't make a fuss but joins his Islander mates out the back, and it is from here that he first catches sight of the woman he will eventually marry. He runs after her and calls out to her to join them, but she refuses.

In this short chapter, the focus is on Eddie's early contact with Bonita (Netta), his future wife. Their first proper meeting, when Eddie approaches her at her cousin's wedding, is sweet, as both appear shy, but it is quickly marred when Eddie accidentally drops a bottle of rum he has brought with him. Netta has already told him that she doesn't like alcohol, and Eddie (although slightly intoxicated at the time) has agreed. In fact, the reason Netta wouldn't speak to Eddie when he called out to her in the street was that he had been at the pub and she was worried he might be drunk. Although alcohol consumption is not a central issue in the narrative, there are several occasions where alcohol is a factor in disagreements between Eddie and Netta. This dialogue between them foreshadows these later conflicts.

As the chapter concludes, we see Eddie reading a dictionary – a sign of his determination to educate and inform himself about the world around him. His friend Davy teases him about reading, asking what the point is, saying, 'Blackfella job, that's all you're gonna get.' Davy later expresses his jealousy over Eddie's ability to read and study.

Q The handheld-camera movement as Eddie approaches the wedding allows us to understand his perspective. Another way to do this would be to use a **point-of-view** shot, where what the camera 'sees' is the same as what Eddie is seeing. How do the two techniques differ, in terms of the way we interpret a scene? Why do you think Perkins decided on one and not the other here?

Q Describe how the uses of slow motion in this chapter develop our understanding of characters and their experiences.

Chapter Three (17:02)

Summary: *Eddie and Netta correspond; he visits her at her family's home; they marry and have their first child; they intervene in their neighbours' argument; their child drinks kerosene and, after a trip to the hospital, they can't find a hotel that will allow them a room for the night.*

The courtship between Eddie and Netta is condensed into just a few scenes, with voice-overs of snippets of their letters. After Eddie's first visit to her family, we see him charming local children with origin stories of his home on Murray Island and, equally, charming Netta with similar tales. In his larrikin way, he offers a cheeky addition to the traditional tale, designed to enchant Netta sufficiently that they might share their first kiss. The ploy works, and in the next shot we see them newly married. This chapter exemplifies how large sections of story are conveyed very efficiently and often with little or no dialogue; from their kiss, through to their marriage, the consummation of the marriage and their first few years of life together, barely a word is spoken, but the images – such as their joy when riding away as newlyweds – can tell us a great deal about what is happening.

There are two other important incidents in this chapter. The first is when Eddie and Netta intervene in an argument between Davy and his wife, who live in the house next door. Eddie halts the physical violence, then, while Netta comforts Davy's wife, Eddie and Davy have a brief but revealing conversation. Eddie thinks he understands his friend Davy's frustration, but is surprised to hear that he is actually part of it, when

Davy expresses jealousy: 'I wanna be you. Reading your dictionary, talkin' in the union.' Eddie seems not to have realised the extent of the reputation he has begun to earn: a self-educated man making an impact in the unionised arena of the industrial sector and enjoying some sort of success in the 'whitefella' world.

This conversation is juxtaposed, almost immediately, with the second important incident: the discrimination that Eddie and Netta face when they attempt to find a hotel room after their son is discharged from the hospital. None of Eddie's status (or perceived status) from the union world will help him here; he faces the same attitudes that any Aboriginal or Islander might have faced at this time when looking for a room in a hotel. Eddie decides he has had enough of such treatment, and tells Netta he doesn't want to raise their children in that environment. In the next scene, it is 1976 and they have moved to Townsville – another example of the efficiency of the episodic structure.

Q Eddie says to Davy, 'We all homesick, brother.' What other evidence have we seen so far that shows how Eddie feels about his homeland?

Q How would you describe Eddie and Netta's relationship?

Chapter Four (24:56)

Summary: *A union mate encourages Eddie to raise issues at meetings; he is again denied service at a pub; he quits his job; he and Netta argue over principle and practicality. Archival footage of Indigenous-rights activism concludes the chapter.*

The early part of this chapter offers an interesting juxtaposition of empowerment and discrimination, similar to that in the previous chapter. This time, Eddie is encouraged by a mate to raise the issues he wants to see discussed at the union meetings, instead of asking others to do it: 'If you wanna raise stuff, mate, do it yourself. You've got a voice, haven't ya?' Eddie is excited by this possibility of active involvement.

Key point

For Eddie, the offhand comment from a union mate about raising concerns directly is a turning point. The idea that he has 'a voice' will be central to his activism for many years to come. Until now, he hasn't realised that he might be heard, but from now on he becomes determined to use his voice, his presence, his passion and his knowledge to bring about change and make things better for his family and for others in his position.

Despite Eddie's newfound confidence, the very next sequence shows him again denied service in the pub with workmates. This time he returns with a hand-lettered declaration on a scrap of cardboard: 'I'm not leaving until I get a drink.' He sits at the bar while beer flows freely for the non-Indigenous patrons, his quiet protest to no avail; and because he does not return home in time to mind the children (instead, spending some hours in the local lock-up), Netta has to leave them with a neighbour so she can go to work. We see here that they both have to work hard to support their growing family, and that Eddie's stubborn and passionate activism impacts on their life together – a theme that will recur throughout.

When he finally does return home late that night, Eddie is able to tell Netta with honesty that he 'never had a drop', despite the fact that his *intention* was likely to spend the evening 'groggin' with the communists', behaviour of which she angrily accuses him. Here we see Eddie typically turning the situation to his advantage, using his evening in the lock-up as a way to subtly deceive Netta about his activities.

Eddie's activism, however, is beginning to earn him a reputation, and colleagues at the wharf tell him that people are calling him a communist – not a popular label at the time. Eddie quits his job, citing poor treatment, and goes home to Netta, elated that he has taken control of his destiny. But Netta can't share his glee; instead, her concern for the welfare of their family quickly turns into anger at Eddie's actions. He is filled with ideas about starting an organisation for waterside workers, encouraged by the Aboriginal Advancement League in Cairns. The couple argue passionately about the idea that they can 'make things better', a disagreement that concludes with Netta's threats to leave, with the children, if he doesn't stop 'mixin' with those commos'.

The conflict here shows how different Eddie and Netta's priorities are, and yet, in a sense, they both want the same things: better lives for the people they care about. Netta's focus, however, is on her immediate family, while Eddie has a 'big-picture' perspective and wants to improve conditions for the broader Indigenous and Islander community – and not only right now, but also into the future.

Key vocabulary

Commo: a derogatory nickname for a communist. Communism is a political movement characterised by, among other things, an aspiration towards a society without the divisions of class. Eddie's beliefs in, and activism directed towards, more equal race relations lead others to perceive him as a communist.

Q Why does Netta want Eddie to abstain from his political activism?

Q Do you think Eddie has a 'voice' within his society? Why or why not?

Chapter Five (33:22)

Summary: *It's 1973 and Eddie is working as the gardener at James Cook University when he meets Noel Loos and then Henry Reynolds; Henry warns Eddie of the dangers of activism. We see Netta and Eddie running the school, and Eddie's mother calls from Murray to say that his father is ill.*

In this chapter, Eddie's activism reaches a new level. In Noel Loos and Henry Reynolds, Eddie meets a match for his passion, and for his commitment to self-education and action. Noel and Henry are academics who specialise in Indigenous histories and race relations, and they are thrilled to meet an informed, ardent Islander who can broaden their knowledge with his personal perspective. For Eddie, the burgeoning friendships bring increased access to knowledge and new possibilities for how he might 'make things better' (Chapter Four). Henry notes, however, that activism is 'not an easy path', particularly under the Bjelke-Petersen government. He doesn't try to discourage Eddie, but rather seeks to educate him, so that Eddie's decision to fight for the cause may be informed rather than naive. Henry's commitment to race relations is a long-term struggle, not a hot-headed fight for brief, bright glory.

The other important aspect of this chapter is Eddie and Netta's involvement in the 'black community school' Eddie has set up, and of which he is headmaster. Here we see both of the Mabos' passionate commitment to the education of Indigenous children: in a montage, we see Netta teaching a class to weave baskets, and Eddie driving them home from school. These scenes emphasise two important facts:

- Eddie's commitment to bettering the lives of Indigenous people is practical as well as idealistic – he actively offers concrete improvements even while pursuing philosophical, academic and idealistic activism.
- Eddie and Netta, while they experience conflict over the levels of activism that are reasonable, do still share some of the same passion. This scene shows their mutual joy at the activities of the school, indicating that their relationship is enduring and based on shared values and priorities.

Q How does Eddie's friendship with Henry and Noel change him?

Q What beliefs do Eddie and Netta share? On what values do their opinions differ?

Chapter Six (39:13)

Summary: *The Mabo family is denied permission to visit Murray Island; Eddie debriefs with Noel and Henry, who tell him he doesn't own the land on the island; Eddie makes the decision to fight for the land and to 'make history'; he and his lawyers begin to compile the land-rights claim.*

This is a central chapter in terms of both the political narrative and Eddie's personal journey. After being denied permission by the Murray Island Council to return home and farewell his dying father, Eddie fantasises to Henry and Noel about going 'back home' one day, setting up a shack on the land he has inherited, and living 'the old traditional way'. Henry breaks the news: 'The land's not technically yours. Legally, I mean. The government owns it.' Eddie is stunned and angered to discover this, and vows to fight for the land.

Much of the rest of the chapter is concerned with contextualising the details of the land-rights case that will take place. For example, during a public meeting to discuss the future of Australian race relations, we learn that a previous Indigenous land-rights claim failed, but that 'the High Court found in favour of a form of native title in PNG' (Papua New Guinea). This foreshadows the later High Court challenge, and the eventual rejection of terra nullius. The discussion between several of Eddie's prospective lawyers informs us how important Eddie's case will be, in a much broader sense: Ron Castan tells Bryan Keon-Cohen that his involvement with this case will define the rest of his career – not just 'the kind of briefs you're offered, but, more importantly, the ones you're not'. This is a reminder of how inflammatory the conflicts over race relations at the time could be; firm sides were taken, and allegiances had lasting impacts on people's personal identities, careers and lives.

Key point

In the scene following the public meeting, we see Eddie's ambitions and belief in the importance of his role in the world, as he declares he is 'taking the government to court' and will make history. There is a suggestion that his desire to 'make things better' is almost matched by his desire to achieve a form of glory for himself. Eddie is never portrayed as either a simplistically selfish character or a simplistically altruistic man, but rather as a more complex personality, driven by many needs and hopes.

The legal drama and detail of this chapter is contrasted with scenes of domesticity and socio-academic pursuit, illustrating the relationship between Eddie, Noel and Henry, and, through this friendship, the potential for education to lead to improved race relations. First we see Eddie guest-lecturing in one of Noel's classes, offering a personal perspective on the theoretical teachings. Further personalising the idea of education, when Noel and Henry join the Mabos for dinner, one of Eddie's sons is invited to share with them some of the teachings of the Piaderem (the Mabo clan). We see Eddie's pride that he has been able to teach his son the traditional stories that his own father taught him, and his pleasure at being able – so far from his island – to share this with his non-Islander friends. Again, here, Eddie's recollections of his father's voice overlay the dialogue, and we see flashbacks to the opening scene of Eddie and Benny at the water's edge. This indicates the strength of the links between Eddie's past and present.

Key vocabulary

High Court: the highest court of appeal within the Australian legal system.

Native title: a legal recognition, within the Australian justice system, of Indigenous land ownership. This was brought into effect by the Mabo case.

Terra nullius: a Latin term used in legal discourse to mean land that does not belong to anyone. In the Australian context, it describes the conception that Australia, before European settlement, was uninhabited and without ownership.

Piaderem: the clan to which the Mabos belong; 'the clan of the holy ones', as Benny explains.

Aiet (pronounced 'ite'): traditional leaders in the Meriam culture.

Q How would you define 'land ownership'?

Chapter Seven (48:01)

Summary: *The chapter begins with archival news footage of the public and media response to Eddie's case and the announcement of Joh Bjelke-Petersen's retrospective extinguishment of native title. Eddie visits his lawyers in Melbourne to discuss their plan of attack; both the case and the Mabo family are low on funds and require support. In 1986 the Mabos travel to Murray Island, where the Queensland Supreme Court holds its first sitting on the island. Eddie's nomination for the Murray Island Council is rejected.*

The Mabo land-rights case has barely even begun before Queensland premier Joh Bjelke-Petersen attempts to prevent it, passing an act to retrospectively extinguish native title on Queensland's coastal islands. This indicates that the government recognised the potential for the Mabo case to set a precedent that could impact on many future land-rights claims.

As Eddie prepares to go to Melbourne, he explains to Netta that the Bjelke-Petersen act is 'a law to kill us off': for Eddie, this isn't only about his own land-rights claim, but about the identity, legal recognition and very existence of Indigenous and Torres Strait Islander Australians.

Netta's response is typically concerned with the practicalities: 'You can't keep flying around the country like this – how are we going to pay for it?' We quickly see that her point has validity: when Eddie meets with his lawyers, they inform him that the case is broke and they will need to apply for Legal Aid. This is echoed immediately in the domestic sphere; the next scene shows Eddie collecting government benefits in order to support his family, because the case is interfering with his ability to hold down a job.

Again, we see the tension between the 'big picture' and the smaller. In order to make things better for himself and his people, Eddie often sacrifices his own family's needs, and Netta feels this conflict acutely. She wants to support Eddie in the case, recognising, 'This is big.' But she still prioritises their safety and security as a family.

Finally, in 1986 Eddie returns home to Murray, with Netta; it is her first visit to the island. They are there for the court to hear evidence in the case. This scene is quickly juxtaposed with Eddie's meeting with the Murray Island Council, where they explain that they have rejected his nomination. From their perspective, Eddie has no qualification because he has not lived on Murray for more than thirty years. This foreshadows the evidence later given in the case, that Eddie's connection to the island has not been active for a long time. Instead, in the council's eyes he has been living 'down south ... troublemaking and agitating', while the Islanders have tried to negotiate their relationship with Killoran and live peacefully on their traditional land. To Eddie, it is clear that the case is 'the most important thing that will happen to this island in 200 years', and he is angry that the council doesn't see it the same way. He feels thwarted by their authority in the same way he did when they originally punished him, leading to his exile from the island.

The final image in this chapter is of Eddie and a fellow islander fighting on the beach, demonstrating that Eddie's actions are causing division not only between Indigenous and non-Indigenous people, but also among his own community. Not all on the island are supportive of him – some feel that his case is greedy, selfish and unjustified. Eddie, in this scene, maintains his argument that 'it's not about your land or my land, you bloody idiot', but about a bigger cause. Netta begs the two men to stop, and leaves when they won't, reiterating her reluctance to become involved in Eddie's fights against the world around him.

Q In the news report (at around 53 minutes), Bob Katter, Minister for Aboriginal and Islander Affairs, accuses Eddie of using the land-rights claim as a 'springboard for power'. How would you describe Eddie's motivations for pursuing the case? What evidence does the text offer to support your interpretation?

Chapter Eight (57:42)

Summary: *The Supreme Court case begins; Killoran intimidates George Passi, and Sam and David Passi withdraw as plaintiffs. Legal Aid won't continue to fund the trial, but may fund a test case challenging Bjelke-Petersen's act in the High Court. The Mabo family receive death threats. The High Court finds in favour of Mabo.*

The Supreme Court case offers us a level of detail about Eddie's heritage and family history that we have not yet had access to, such as the fact that Benny Mabo was not Eddie's biological father. It is unusual for this kind of **expository** information to occur so late in the narrative, and it influences the impressions we form of the characters and their relationships. For example, perhaps if we had understood Eddie's biological connection (or lack thereof) to his island home earlier, we might have formed a less empathetic opinion about his land-rights claim. This is an example of how the structure of the story can influence our understanding and responses.

When Eddie hears that the Passi brothers have withdrawn from the case, leaving only himself and James Rice as plaintiffs, he immediately (and correctly) guesses that Killoran has intimidated them. Eddie's understanding of this strategy will serve him well when Killoran attempts a similar manipulation against him later.

We soon discover that the case – which is not going well anyway – has again run out of money: Legal Aid won't continue to fund the trial as it is. However, the attorney-general's office considers it to have merit on a broader level, just as Eddie has always envisaged it would. They are prepared to fund an attempt to challenge the Bjelke-Petersen act regarding native title at a High Court level. Eddie and his lawyers accept the opportunity, and later in the chapter this is rewarded when the High Court decision is handed down in their favour, finding the act unconstitutional.

During this time, Netta tells Eddie that they have received death threats over the phone. Eddie orders her to take the children and go away for a while, but Netta refuses, stubbornly and angrily, demonstrating her strength and determination to protect their family and keep them together. We see here that Netta and Eddie are well matched in their commitment to what they believe in, even when they show it in different ways.

Q What is the impact of withholding information about Eddie's history (such as the fact that Benny Mabo was not his biological father)?

Chapter Nine (1:07:06)

Summary: *Eddie and Netta remember the past; the court case provides evidence that Eddie did know about his biological heritage when he was young; Eddie and Netta argue; Netta leaves with the children.*

Eddie and Netta sit up late at night, reminiscing about their first meeting, reminding us that *Mabo* is not only a story of politics, race and history, but also of a love that endures many challenges. This scene is followed by another courtroom scene, demonstrating that the love and the politics are never very far apart.

Killoran's attempt to intimidate Eddie into withdrawing his claim – just as the Passi brothers did – and Eddie's refusal to comply show us his stubbornness and determination. He doesn't hesitate to continue the case, even though things are not looking promising for him, and the trial continues to turn up evidence against his claim, painting him as a greedy and disingenuous man.

At home, Eddie continues to be preoccupied with the case at the expense of his family, and when he and Netta argue about it, he resorts to violence – he is about to hit her when one of the children intervenes. Netta leaves in the middle of the night with the children.

Q During the court scenes, whose side of the case do you sympathise with? Why?

Q How does this chapter argue for the importance of family?

Chapter Ten (1:16:00)

Summary: *Eddie brings his family home; Dave Passi returns as a plaintiff; Eddie loses his land-rights case; the plaintiffs decide to take the issue to the High Court.*

When Eddie quietly comes to collect Netta and the children (perhaps the next morning), she is still angry but is also ready to come home with him before he even asks, indicating that their relationship is important to both of them, and stronger than the challenges they face. When he gently reaches for her arm, she pulls away, saying 'bruise there' – a reminder of the conflict between them, and her way of saying that although she loves him, he has hurt her and she can't forget that.

An idyllic domestic scene follows, with Eddie fishing and digging root vegetables, and then preparing the food with his children, suggesting his repentance and his desire to support the family in the way that Netta would like him to. However, in the next scene Eddie is leaving on a bus to return to the court case, focusing again on what he is so passionate about.

Key point

On the bus, Eddie takes several tablets. As with many other aspects of the narrative, an important detail (his illness) is hinted at in a very brief, dialogue-free image. We will not know more about his illness until later.

The return of Dave Passi as a plaintiff provides new hope for the case, and they share a tender moment of reconciliation before the court scenes continue. However, when the case concludes, Justice Moynihan finds in favour of the Passi but not the Mabo claim. Eddie is faced with a choice: whether to appeal his own case, or to pursue it to the High Court in a case that will be 'about all the blackfellas'. This is a moment where we see Eddie's passion not only for his own justice but also for the cause in which he believes. He is keen to know that his name will still be on the case – the personal glory is important to him – but he does not hesitate to choose the broader cause over a possibility of winning his own land claim.

Q How does this scene contribute to our perception of Eddie as a selfish or a selfless man?

Chapter Eleven (1:26:00)

Summary: *Eddie and Netta go to Canberra for the High Court case; Eddie is diagnosed with cancer; they await the High Court's decision.*

The opening scene in this chapter shows Eddie alone, late at night, gazing at one of his sketches of Murray Island. Netta, unseen by Eddie, watches him. This concise image symbolises several important ideas in the narrative, such as:

- Eddie's constant and often lonely determination
- Eddie's enduring love for his homeland, even though it is often a distant image or an ideal rather than a concrete reality
- Netta's quiet and sometimes unacknowledged presence and support.

This image is followed by a single, short shot of Eddie rubbing his back – another hint of his illness.

Eddie and Netta raise money through donations to go to Canberra for the High Court case, and as they sit in the court while the case begins, the image of Netta clasping Eddie's hand accompanies the audio of the court proceedings. This is a strong symbol of how Eddie's love for his wife and family underlies his political passion for his land.

While they await the High Court's deliberations, we see Eddie in increasing pain, and Netta insists that he visit more doctors. Eddie makes a tearful apology to Netta for not spending more time with the family over the years. The tone of sorrowful regret hints that he is nearing the end of his life, looking back and appraising his decisions, and realising the impact of his political activism on his personal life.

A diagnosis of cancer follows, and as the High Court judges continue to study the case, Netta brings Eddie to hospital, where he lies, drifting between the present reality and his imagined landscape of his island home. In narrative terms, the decline in Eddie's health is very fast, and it is conveyed, like many other important plot developments, primarily through images: Eddie in his hospital bed surrounded by his children; Netta holding his hand while he sleeps; a flashback to him smiling in the doorway at their first meeting; Eddie sitting by the water writing a note to 'them up on Murray' as his family walk on without him.

Q What does the music throughout this chapter contribute to the narrative or to our understanding of what is happening – or what might be soon to happen?

Chapter Twelve (1:36:10)

Summary: *The High Court finds in favour of Mabo; there is a flashback to Eddie awaiting the High Court decision before his death; captions summarise the subsequent events.*

In this final, short chapter, we see the result of Eddie and his family's long struggle as the High Court judges deliver their findings, which overwhelmingly support not only Eddie's claim but also the notion that non-Indigenous settlement has inflicted great injustice on Indigenous peoples.

Significantly, none of the Mabos are present when the decision is handed down: Netta and one of her sons are listening with a non-Indigenous couple, who offer the use of their radio at their campsite (after the Mabo car ran out of petrol on the way), and Eddie, as we will discover shortly, had died just months before.

The absence of the family from the court at the announcement illustrates the fact that the court case was not just about a single person. Although Eddie has been central to the case all along, the victory is no longer simply about the Mabos but about the Australian community as a whole, as 'the legal existence of Aborigines prior to white settlement' has now been recognised for the first time.

When the decision is reported on the radio, Netta and her son share warm, emotional, celebratory embraces with the strangers at their caravan, representing the potential for future reconciliation between Indigenous and non-Indigenous Australians.

This scene is followed by a kind of epilogue: a flashback to the previous scene in which the Mabos walk away from Eddie at the river; only this time we hear Eddie's letter in voice-over as Netta watches him writing it. He speaks of his great love for her, and of how it has endured and overcome all the challenges of his activist life. Once again, we are reminded of the two parallel themes of Eddie's life: his political passions and his love for family.

Q The telemovie concludes with archival footage of Eddie Mabo's burial on Murray Island. How does this influence our interpretation of the story?

Q If you could write one paragraph to include with the closing subtitles to the film, what would it say? Would you add further historical information about the characters and events, or would you focus on the family relationships? Would you mention what happened to more minor characters, or outline recent legal developments influenced by the Mabo case? Give reasons for your answer.

CHARACTERS & RELATIONSHIPS

Koiki 'Eddie' Mabo

Key quotes

'Whitefellas' name Eddie, but it's Koiki for real.'

'All them say it, on the railway: "Koiki's the one".' (Davy)

'Eddie Mabo is a smooth talker. Always was.' (Killoran)

'Eddie Mabo is … quite capable of tailoring his story to whatever shape he perceived would advance his cause in the particular forum.' (Justice Moynihan)

'You always were one to get above yourself, Eddie.' (Killoran)

'I'm gonna make history. I am the son of Benny Mabo. I am a Meriam man from the Piaderem clan. I am the descendant of the Aiet, and the zogo le. And I'm gonna make history.'

Eddie Mabo, born 29 June 1936, is a Torres Strait Islander from Murray (Mer) Island. Although he leaves the island as a young man – to avoid a punishment handed down by the Murray Island Council – he always feels a connection to his land and heritage, and intends to return there, bringing his wife and children back to his family land. When he learns that the Australian government legally owns the land, he embarks on a long crusade towards regaining the ownership he had assumed he already had. The legal battle requires that Eddie commit himself fully to his fight, sometimes neglecting his family in the process, though he regularly says that his fight is for the betterment of conditions and rights for all of his people. In this way, he is caring for his children's future in the only way he understands: by fighting for what he believes belongs to them, according to Meriam cultural tradition and law.

Eddie is proud of his heritage – he is a descendant of an important Mer clan, as well as the Aiet (traditional leaders) and the zogo le (individuals with special powers, associated with Malo, the octopus spirit or god of the island). His connection to these ancestors is through his adoption into the Mabo family and not through bloodlines, but this makes no difference to him. He has little or no association with his birth family throughout *Mabo*, and his self-identified heritage is the one for which he fights.

A proud and passionate man defined by his political activism, Eddie dies tragically, just before the announcement of the High Court decision in his favour.

Key point

Although the character and the real Koiki 'Eddie' Mabo share much in common, the character is a particular representation or interpretation of the real man, and the two should not be confused.

Family man

Although the political battles Eddie fights are the central issues in his life, he is also father to a growing family and a loving wife to Netta. There are numerous occasions in which we see Eddie's commitment to his family, including:

- His decision to leave western Queensland when their first child is young, in order to raise him in a better place (Chapter Three).
- His anger and sadness when he is denied permission to return to Murray Island with his family to farewell his dying father (Chapter Six).
- His suggestion to Netta that she take the children and leave for a while, after they receive death threats (Chapter Eight).
- His efforts to be the father and provider Netta would like him to be (Chapter Ten).
- His regretful apology to Netta for not spending more time with them, and his joy at seeing them when they visit him in hospital (Chapter Eleven).
- His letter, which we hear during the flashback in Chapter Twelve, describing how much he loves Netta.

These examples remind us that although Eddie's activism and legal battles are the focus of the narrative, he is not a one-dimensional character who is used merely to tell the story of the native title court case, but rather a complex man who is trying to balance the various values and beliefs in his life.

'Cheeky Koiki'

When Netta first meets Eddie, he tells her his 'whitefellas' name' is Eddie but 'it's Koiki for real', and Netta responds, 'Koiki. Sounds cheeky. Cheeky Koiki' (Chapter Two). We see many instances of Eddie's 'cheeky' behaviour: as Justice Moynihan observes, Eddie is not afraid to twist the rules or even the truth in order to achieve the best outcome for himself. Examples include:

- Eddie sends his friend Davy to complete the railway medical for him, so that he can pass the eye test and work in western Queensland (Chapter One).
- When Eddie meets Netta at her cousin's wedding, he agrees with her statement 'I don't like drink', even though he is intoxicated, in order to make her like him more (Chapter Two).
- He tells Netta that he 'never had a drop' of alcohol on the evening he was sent to the lock-up for the night – the statement is only true because the barman had refused to serve him (Chapter Four).

Eddie's 'cheekiness' rarely gets him into trouble, but rather tends to endear him to others. This has echoes of a familiar character in Australian literature and culture: the 'larrikin'. The word, while originally (and sometimes still) derogatory, is often used affectionately, to describe someone both mischievous and good-hearted, and denotes a certain level of respect for those who stand up against authorities or established conventions.

Pride and confidence

Eddie's pride regarding his heritage, rights and abilities is often what sets him apart from those around him. It affords him a confidence to take important actions, including:

- He leaves the island to find a job instead of accepting the Murray Island Council's punishment.
- He joins the union, recruiting other Islanders, and maintains an active presence in the union.
- He pursues legal battles throughout his life.

Pride can be considered a valuable trait because it suggests passion and sparks action, but it can also often lead to, or be interpreted as, arrogance – such as when Eddie tells the woman at the unemployment benefits office that he couldn't possibly be expected to work for a living while he is in the middle of suing the government (Chapter Seven). His pride in his entitlement to the large quantity of land on Murray Island is also seen as arrogance: some fellow Islanders think his claim is greedy (Chapter Seven), and when his claim is denied but the Passi claim supported, his lawyers admit that he may have tried to ask for too much land and make too much of his connection to the island's traditional leadership (Chapter Ten). Eddie articulates the fact that this made him look 'greedy' in the eyes of the judge.

Bryan Keon-Cohen also notes that Eddie is 'too articulate': 'He'd read too much. He was just too smart.' This, ironically, makes him less likeable for some people, rather than more.

Eddie's confidence does sometimes seem unjustified: in the face of multiple losses in the various court cases, despite repeatedly running out of money and regardless of the seemingly impossible odds to overcome, Eddie only ever believes that he can win. He won't accept the possibility of failure, and in response to anyone's doubt, he repeats over and over that he will succeed:

- To a member of the Murray Island Council, who asks, 'What happens if you don't win?', he says firmly, 'I will win it. We will win' (Chapter Seven).
- To a friendly neighbour who enquires about the progress of the case, he says calmly, 'We're gonna win it. No doubt about it' (Chapter Ten).

- To Netta, when she dares to ask, in exhaustion and frustration, what they will do if he doesn't win, he responds angrily, threatening violence against her and the children, 'if that's what I need to do to earn respect' (Chapter Nine).

His confidence is unshakeable, and while that is what drives and bolsters him to ultimately succeed at the High Court level, it is also something that causes conflict and difficulty for him in his interactions with others.

Q Identify some other 'larrikin' figures in contemporary Australian culture and literature, film and television. Why are these characters likeable? When do we condemn instead of value mischievous behaviour? Does Eddie get away with his behaviour because of his larrikin nature?

Q Do the events of *Mabo* endorse pride as a positive value, or condemn it as a quality to be avoided?

Netta

Key quotes

'She's not from Murray, but she's willing to come back. We've got a plan, her and me.' (Eddie)

'I reckon that's the moment I fell in love with you, even before I knew you was gonna make history.'

'I'm not going … I'm getting in this bed, same as I've done every night for thirty years.'

Netta is loyal, stubborn, strong, practical, hard-working, and values the wellbeing of her family above anything else. We know little of her background or life before or beyond her marriage. She works nights – even while heavily pregnant – at a local prawn factory to help support the family. She is proud of Eddie, and shares his views about Indigenous and Islander rights. This aspect of Netta's character is shown on several occasions, including the following:

- When Netta argues with Eddie after he quits his job, she admits that she had engaged in her own tiny act of protest while being served after all the white people.
- She participates in running the community school with Eddie, teaching traditional skills to the children.
- Netta marches in a protest with Eddie (in the re-enacted version of archival footage at the end of Chapter Four).

However, Netta is not proud of fighting for the cause to the same degree that Eddie is, and seems to subscribe to the old adage 'charity begins at home'. While she accepts Eddie's passions, and supports him throughout his life, she is angered whenever the activism impacts on the welfare of their family. For example, when he quits his job, she is furious because she doesn't know how they will afford to feed their children. The same issue recurs later: when Eddie wants to go to Melbourne to meet with the lawyers, she worries about him missing days at work, and about how they will pay for the flights.

Strength

Netta is not afraid of hard work; nor is she easily spooked by the challenges that Eddie's activism sometimes poses. For example, when the family receive death threats, Eddie's immediate response is to send her and the children away, for their protection. She objects, saying that she isn't going anywhere (Chapter Eight). She is aware of the danger, but isn't going to run away from it.

Similarly, when Eddie's frustration about the case leads to a one-off incident of near-abuse, she calmly takes the children away under cover of darkness, and just as calmly returns when Eddie, quietly repentant, comes to collect them. This demonstrates her love for him, and her confidence that she can look after herself and her children, while maintaining her relationship with Eddie.

Q Do Netta's beliefs and values change throughout her life with Eddie? If so, how? If not, why do you think they remain the same?

Netta and Eddie

Key quotes

Eddie: People like us have no choice but to be troublemakers. Cause if we don't, we don't have any pride left.

Netta: I'll give you stinkin' pride. You got three kids, stupid man. Fourth on the way. Healthy, happy kids. What more do you want?

'… my wife, the most important person in my life, has stuck to me, over many hardships and hurdles, but somehow we made it. My wife has been the most adorable person, a friend closest in my life …' (Eddie)

'And we loved every minute of our lives together.' (Eddie)

Eddie meets Netta early in the story and their courtship is conducted in less than five minutes of screen time. Their relationship is central to the story and provides a domestic counterpoint to the political themes. Although they share values, the two differ significantly in their approaches to life.

Priorities

The text does not explore in detail how or why the central characters have formed their particular views. For example, we know very little about Netta's background before she meets Eddie. Rather than spending time analysing the development of such qualities, the telemovie instead explores in detail where their views differ, and the impact of this on their relationship.

Netta takes her family, and her responsibilities as a mother, very seriously. While she supports Eddie, she is forever tempering his idealism with a dose of practicality, always reminding him that while he fights for the rights of a community, she will fight for the rights of their children. When they argue, this is what they argue about: Eddie believes he must pursue his legal battles, while Netta reminds him that he is a father as well as a political activist. When he explains that without rights they have no pride, she reminds him, 'Kids gotta be fed, gotta have clothes on their back' (Chapter Four). When he rails against the unfair image the opposing lawyers have presented of him, Netta furiously reminds him that 'these kids, they've been living on frozen fish and flour for nine years' while the case has held his attention (Chapter Nine).

Where Eddie's idealism drives him to focus on the legal battles instead of on the daily grind of life, Netta's pragmatism forces her to concentrate on day-to-day survival. Eddie wants the best for his family and his people, but in his broad view he forgets the detail; Netta wants the best for her family, and in trying to support them, she sometimes loses sight of the 'big picture'.

Key point

In many ways, Netta and Eddie serve as foils for each other, providing evidence of opposing approaches to life even though they share values and love for each other.

Mabo endorses both philosophies – the micro and the macro approaches – and shows that neither can succeed alone. It is only with each other's support that Eddie and Netta live a happy life and raise children who have positive futures ahead of them.

Enduring love

Although we frequently see Eddie and Netta in situations of conflict – usually revolving around the legal battles – we also realise that their love is important to both of them. Netta stands behind Eddie through all the legal challenges and is at his bedside during his last days, and in Eddie's final voice-over, we hear how important this support has been to him.

Eddie makes a joke at the end of Chapter Five that reminds us that for him, love and politics are never far apart. He tells Netta she's forgotten it is the anniversary. She assumes he's referring to their anniversary (indicating that their relationship is the most important thing to her), but he says he was teasing, and in fact referring to the anniversary of the community school opening (indicating that, once again, politics and activism are his main concern). Despite their different priorities, both laugh and begin to plan a 'celebration' they will enjoy together, indicating the strength of their love for each other.

Q How do you think Netta and Eddie's lives would have changed if she had left him, as she sometimes threatened to do?

Q Is Netta's character defined solely by her relationship with Eddie? Justify your answer with evidence from the text.

Patrick Killoran

Key quotes

'You're too young, too hot-headed, and I protect you from yourself.'

'Joh's been hurt by this ... the way he sees it, and I've got to agree, is he's got you blackfellas out from under the act, and how'd you pay him back? Turned around and spit in his face with all this land rights nonsense.'

Killoran, the government-appointed 'Protector' of the Torres Strait Islanders on Murray Island, holds great power over Eddie and his community. Although Killoran is a minor character, he appears regularly at critical points in Eddie's life, both on Murray Island and on mainland Australia. For example, it is Killoran who first informs Eddie that the council has decided to exile him in punishment for his youthful transgression (Chapter One), offering him the less-than-attractive alternative of working without pay on the rubbish truck. Eddie resents Killoran's control and attitude – although Killoran is a nominative 'protector', he seems to take pleasure in making the Islanders' lives harder. On many occasions we see Killoran use bullying tactics, including:

- when he hints that Eddie won't make it on his own if he goes to work for the Queensland railway (Chapter One)
- when he discourages George Passi and his brothers from being involved in the Mabo case (Chapter Eight)
- when he tries to get Eddie to withdraw the case (Chapter Nine).

On each of these occasions, Killoran attempts to intimidate the Islanders. For example, he tells George how the family could lose money, and threatens to withdraw his support from the community; and he tries to make Eddie feel guilty about how his father – and indeed the whole Murray community – would feel about the case: 'If Benny were alive today, how would he feel watching you make this big a fool of the Mabo name? ... Watching you ... stuff everything up, for everyone?'

Killoran represents the power that the government had over Indigenous people at this time.

Q Do you think that Killoran has the best interests of his Indigenous charges at heart, or does he use his power selfishly? What evidence from the telemovie supports your view?

Q In what ways are Eddie and Killoran alike?

Noel Loos and Henry Reynolds

Key quotes

Noel: The Cambridge expedition, 1898. What did you make of it?

Eddie: ... most of it's rubbish.

Noel: Something we both agree on.

Henry: So, you have an interest in Indigenous issues?

Eddie: [*laughs*] Where do you want to start?

Noel teaches Aboriginal history and anthropology, and Henry is a historian specialising in Aboriginal history. They meet Eddie while he is working at James Cook University as a gardener, and are instrumental in enabling his activism. Their relationship with Eddie is symbiotic (beneficial to both parties): they are able to broaden his knowledge from their academic perspective, and he is able to enrich their learning with his first-person experience of some of the cultural issues they have long wrestled with from intellectual, political and theoretical perspectives.

In a world where there is little evidence of friendship or social networks for the Mabo family, Henry and Noel become friends to Eddie, as well as colleagues and advocates. This is evidenced in scenes such as that in Chapter Six, when the men share dinner with Eddie and his family in the Mabo home.

Key point

Henry and Noel are central to the plot, as they provide Eddie with the information that he doesn't legally own the land on Murray Island. This is a turning point, when his activism becomes focused and specific.

Greg McIntyre, Barbara Hocking, Ron Castan and Bryan Keon-Cohen

Key quotes

'It's been pretty clear to a number of us for a while now that it might be time to revisit the land-rights issue ... To our Indigenous friends we say this: now is your time.' (Greg)

'You're gonna have to think very carefully, Bryan. It'll pretty much shape the rest of your career.' (Ron)

Eddie first meets Greg McIntyre and Barbara Hocking, of the Aboriginal Legal Service in Cairns, in 1981 at a public lecture entitled 'Land Rights and the Future of Australian Race Relations' (Chapter Six). During this lecture the lawyers discuss a High Court finding in favour of a native title claim in Papua New Guinea, and suggest that it may form a precedent and the time is ripe for a new effort at achieving legal recognition for Indigenous land-rights claims. This event occurs just after Eddie's discovery that he doesn't legally own the land, and he is passionate and ready to fight for his cause: the opportunity has arisen at just the right moment. He and Dave Passi speak excitedly with them after the lecture, full of the possibility of success.

As with Noel and Henry, the lawyers, too, benefit from Eddie's involvement as much as he benefits from theirs, in that he is a willing plaintiff in a case that allows them to pursue a fundamental legal issue that they have been waiting to tackle. The lawyers have the expertise Eddie needs, and he has the energy and personal involvement they need.

Greg and Barbara recruit Ron and Bryan, Melbourne lawyers with interests and expertise in human-rights and Indigenous issues, who have been waiting for just the right case. As Ron says when inviting Bryan to come on board, 'I think this might be the one' (Chapter Six). They are seen to fight tirelessly for Eddie's cause – we know from Ron and Bryan's first conversation that there is no money in the case for them, and they run out of funds several times, so their motivation is clearly something other than financial success. As Ron reminds Bryan, their involvement is also likely to lose them many other big briefs, such as with mining companies or with the government.

Eddie's lawyers, like Eddie, appear to be 'fighting the good fight' – dedicating themselves to a human-rights cause for the good of all Indigenous Australians. But, as with Eddie's situation, they also stand to reap great personal gain from the success of the case, which will bring recognition and secure them a place in the history books. *Mabo* portrays these characters positively: they are patient, passionate, respectful, and stand for values such as justice and equality. But the script is quite careful about not canonising (making saints out of) them. Rather, it presents them as hard-working individuals who are fighting for what they believe in.

Q What do you think motivates the lawyers working on Eddie's case – are they seeking glory or purely justice?

THEMES, IDEAS & VALUES

Equality and discrimination

Key quotes

'What – they think we're gonna leave our black skin on their bloody sheets?' (Eddie)

'It's not me, it's the law.' (barman who refuses to serve Eddie)

'We believe the High Court has been holding this window open for years ... if we delay any longer, we'll lose the moment and set the whole cause back another decade.' (Ron)

Mabo represents a historical 'moment': a very recent point in Australia's social and cultural history where changes in legal recognition of Indigenous land entitlement reflected, and perhaps shaped, corresponding changes in attitudes, assumptions and relations between Indigenous and non-Indigenous Australians. Certainly the Mabo decision was not unanimously welcomed, and many years later, unfair discrimination (unequal treatment based on prejudices against a particular person or group) still exists, but the High Court decision was, as Prime Minister Paul Keating described it at the time, 'an historic decision'. He continued to express the hope that Australians could 'make it an historic turning point, the basis of a new relationship between Indigenous and non-Aboriginal Australians' (Chapter Twelve). It was a significant shift not only in public policy, but also in public perception of Indigenous Australians' relationship with land, and of the rights and responsibilities of settler Australians. The telemovie portrays this event, illustrating it with Eddie's life and his experiences of inequality as an Indigenous man.

In *Mabo*, we see numerous instances of discrimination against Eddie and his family and fellow Islanders, including the following:

- Patrick Killoran regularly uses his government-given power to unfairly discriminate against his charges, bullying and intimidating them and maintaining control over their lives on the grounds that they are not capable of looking after themselves. This is a reminder that discrimination can occur at both personal and administrative levels.
- After their son's hospital visit, no hotel will rent Eddie and Netta a room (Chapter Three). Although the hotel owners claim that they are full up, Eddie and Netta's responses suggest that this rejection is based on the colour of their skin and not the availability of rooms.
- Eddie is twice refused service in pubs with his workmates (Chapters Two and Four).
- Netta describes her anger at being served after all the white people in line (Chapter Four), and this is closely followed by the archival footage documenting such discrimination.

We do also see some instances of 'equal' treatment for Eddie, where his racial identity does not determine interactions. One clear example is in Chapter Four, when a colleague tells him that he has a voice, and should raise the issues he wants to discuss at union meetings, instead of relying on his non-Indigenous peers. We see how this notion empowers Eddie, as he begins to take on a more active role in the unions, and eventually in his own legal case.

Key point

The rare illustrations of equality in the text serve to highlight the impacts of an *absence* of equal treatment.

Despite occasional experiences of equality, discriminatory treatment is so familiar to Eddie that when he first meets Noel Loos he is on the defensive and immediately assumes that Noel is being judgemental and racist. This demonstrates the long-term psychological impacts that discrimination can have, and the extent to which it will affect an individual's perception of the world around them: Eddie's initial response to Noel was negative, and could easily have prevented the beneficial and positive friendship that ensues. Their first exchange occurs in Chapter Five, when, after observing him reading in the library, Noel seeks Eddie out:

> NOEL: Have I seen you in the library?
>
> EDDIE: You may have. There's no law against that, is there?
>
> NOEL: Just unusual to see a gardener in the library.
>
> EDDIE: You mean it's unusual to see a blackfella in the library.
>
> NOEL: Ah, no, ah ... let's ... let's start again.

Noel has no intention of treating Eddie unfairly; rather, he is interested in getting to know him, understanding his experience and opinions, perhaps broadening his knowledge and potential, and ultimately becoming a friend. And yet, his first meeting with Eddie still reveals his assumptions about particular groups of people: even if he isn't judging Eddie as an Indigenous man, he is still making assumptions about the interests and capacities of gardeners (a particular group of people likely to be lower in the socioeconomic scale than he, an academic) by saying that he doesn't expect to see them in the library. This illustrates a lack of social equality and also, indirectly, a lack of racial equality since, as Eddie's second comment in the above dialogue implies, the socioeconomic parallels between 'gardener' and 'blackfella' are obvious.

This incident demonstrates how easily racial discrimination can take place, even when individuals have the best of intentions. *Mabo*, then, suggests that even people with good intentions can treat each other unfairly: it does not paint a simplistic portrait in which discrimination is limited to 'villainous' or unsympathetic characters. In fact, both Eddie and Noel discriminate against each other during their first meeting. Noel is surprised by Eddie's capacity and inclination to engage with academic material in the library, while Eddie, conversely, has made an assumption

– based on Noel's non-Indigenous status – that Noel's motivations for approaching him must be discriminatory.

The events of the telemovie demonstrate that by moving beyond discrimination and forming friendships based on respect and the equal exchange of information (such as the relationship between Eddie, Henry and Noel eventually exemplifies), challenges can be overcome and great things can be achieved. In this way, the text endorses the notions that discrimination is damaging and that people should strive to treat one another with fairness and equality.

Q Can you identify other instances (not race-based) of unfair discrimination in *Mabo*?

Q How do you think Eddie might describe the idea of 'equality'? How about Netta? Justice Moynihan? How do *you* define it?

Activism

Key quotes

'It's not an easy path, Eddie, the road of the activist.' (Henry)

'Can't stop now. Might as well curl up and die.' (Eddie)

'... all your troublemaking and agitating ...' (Murray Island councillor)

'What more can they do to me that hasn't already been done? I've lost jobs, I've been in the stinkin' lock-up. What more can they do?' (Eddie)

'Fight to make things better'

For Eddie, a natural progression from the experience of discrimination is to engage in activism (strong and active commitment to a cause, usually a political cause). Eddie's early activism is developed through his union involvement, as he begins to participate and to recruit others, speaking up about the need for representation and training for Indigenous workers. We see how his input is valued and respected both by union superiors and by his peers – an example is when Davy expresses his envy at Eddie's knowledge and ability to speak at union meetings, 'talkin' big words I never even heard of'. Yet this is the only way Eddie can see to make a difference to the lives of workers, particularly those who are Indigenous.

Eddie quits his job when he feels that his treatment is becoming increasingly unfair. He begins to take his union activism more seriously, and to take it beyond his workplace: he sees how it can serve his people in the same way it has served his fellow workers. Eddie is filled with zeal, energy and inspiration about the cause, imagining the things they can do to change lives:

> EDDIE: We gotta get together. That's how the union get things done. They get *together*. They lobby, they fundraise and they *fight* to make things better.
>
> NETTA: How you reckon we're gonna do all this, make all this stuff better?
>
> EDDIE: Any way we can!

'Troublemaking and agitating'

While *Mabo* appears to advocate activism (Eddie, after all, is the central figure of the story, and it celebrates his life and achievements as a passionate activist), it also presents opposing views, such as Netta's. While Netta believes in some of the same values as Eddie, such as that Indigenous people should have the right to fair treatment, she is reluctant to fight for them, because she sees the negative impacts such activism can have on their family. For example, there are financial impacts when Eddie is too caught up in his political battles to hold down a job, and there are domestic implications when he decides to stand up for his rights at any cost – such as when he stages the silent protest at the pub, and Netta is forced to leave their children with a neighbour all night while she goes to work.

Activism can sometimes be seen as troublemaking. For example, the Murray Island Council is unwilling to welcome Eddie not only because has he not lived there for over thirty years, but also because while off the island he has been causing trouble and agitating loudly for change, and they don't condone such disruptive behaviour. Instead, they would prefer he had stayed quietly at home on his island and negotiated with Killoran (and thus the government), as they have been attempting to do.

Killoran later intimidates George Passi in order to discourage the Passi brothers' involvement in Eddie's case. Killoran implies that he has been trying to do positive things for the Islanders, such as getting houses painted and schools funded, but that if they cause trouble, such support will be withdrawn. He also describes Eddie's behaviour as making 'a fool of the Mabo name' (Chapter Nine), implying that Eddie should keep quiet and not cause trouble.

These examples illustrate Henry's warning to Eddie: that activism is never easy. But, as we see from the positive outcomes of Eddie's activism – the ultimate changes to constitutional interpretation and land-rights entitlements – the text suggests that though activism may be very difficult, it is entirely necessary in order to bring about change and improve lives.

Q Do you think there is any other way Eddie could have achieved his goals, if not through political activism?

Q Is activism simply stirring up trouble, or is it an important tool for social change? How does *Mabo* support your answer?

Idealism and pragmatism

Key quotes

'I know we're broke, and it feels like we've achieved precisely nothing. But what we're doing here, it's monumental. Let's keep a hold of that.' (Ron)

Netta: What about work?

Eddie: How am I gonna go to work when all of this is going on, woman? Use your brains!

Another notion related to both equality and activism is idealism: believing in and pursuing ideals of how the world *could* be, rather than how it is; striving for something better. Idealism could be considered a motivating value that underlies, justifies or feeds activism. Eddie's passionate, idealistic beliefs that life can be much better for Indigenous people are what drives his commitment to fighting for change.

As discussed in 'Characters and relationships', Eddie and Netta differ markedly in their philosophical approaches to life. Eddie is nearly always driven by idealism, and Netta by pragmatism (an attention to concrete goals and concerns). This allows the text to present both the benefits and downfalls of each approach. The couple argue about Eddie's beliefs after he quits his job:

> NETTA: People like us, we can't afford to be troublemakers.
>
> EDDIE: Netta. People like us have no choice but to *be* troublemakers! Cause if we don't, we don't have any pride left.

This debate illustrates perfectly the tension between the two philosophies. The text also suggests that both perspectives are valid: the Mabo family do not have the financial or social support to throw away their jobs, and yet without change to the rights of Indigenous people, their prospects can never improve.

Mabo clearly shows that both idealism and pragmatism are important, and, indeed, that – as we see in Eddie and Netta's marriage – each one must be balanced with the other in order to have value.

Q What does the text suggest might be the result of a life lived with idealism but no pragmatism? What about pragmatism with no idealism?

Q How would you describe Eddie's ideals?

Q Which view do you feel most empathy with – pragmatism or idealism? Why?

Ownership

Key quotes

'Everything here is yours.' (Benny, to Eddie)

'We've got a system of land ownership and inheritance. We cultivate the land. The links are ... active and unbroken.' (Eddie)

'What about our law? What about Meriam law?' (Eddie)

'Eddie, you know the land's not technically yours? Legally, I mean. The government owns it.' (Henry)

'If anyone tries to tell me that I don't own that land, I'm gonna walk into Killoran's office with a shotgun.' (Eddie)

Ownership – specifically land ownership – is a central issue in *Mabo*. Within the first two minutes of the story, we see Eddie being told that the land around him on Murray Island belongs to him. It is not until much later that this belief is challenged: firstly by Henry Reynolds and Noel Loos, who explain to Eddie the Australian ownership laws, and secondly during the court case, when we learn that Benny was not Eddie's biological father, thus calling into question the heritable entitlement for which Eddie has always argued. There are also other challenges to his belief in his rightful ownership – such as that from a fellow Islander who thinks Eddie's claims are greedy and unjustified (Chapter Seven).

The conflict between Meriam and European–Australian law underpins the land-rights claim: Eddie owns land according to the Meriam law of inheritance and family connection, but not according to the Queensland government. The differing beliefs about the meaning of ownership fuel this struggle, and the text does not offer easy answers; it suggests that there is no one definition of what it means to own land.

Several scenes, including some of the evidence presented and argued in court, offer examples of the different ways in which land ownership may be conceptualised. An excellent example is in the middle of

Chapter Six, when Eddie presents a guest lecture for some of Noel and Henry's students. After he has explained the traditional Malo's laws, the following exchange takes place:

> STUDENT: So you reckon you own the land because some giant octopus said you do?
>
> EDDIE: My people were on those islands for sixteen generations. You think some whitefella sticking a Union Jack in the sand wipes out sixteen generations?

This conversation illustrates how different the notions of land ownership can be between cultures.

After the discussion of Malo's laws continues over the Mabo dinner table with Noel and Henry, a short scene with Barbara Hocking echoes these differing cultural perceptions. She details why a previous native title case – effectively the first – failed, explaining that the judge had found that 'a nomadic people' could not 'demonstrate any traditional property right that could be recognised by Anglo-Australian law'. This suggests that incompatible understandings of land ownership had long existed between Indigenous and non-Indigenous Australians, and sets up a strong motivation for Eddie's legal challenge to prove that he has a right to his land, not just under Meriam but also under Australian law.

Key point

The scenes in Chapter Six illustrate the challenges at the heart of the land-rights claims: how can two such differing legal systems exist and function side by side?

Q What are some of the definitions of 'ownership' this text offers? How else might you define 'ownership'?

Q Eddie claims he owns his land on Murray Island 'as much as we own this house' (in Queensland). What are the different conceptions of 'ownership' being illustrated here?

Family

Key quotes

> 'I wish I'd spent more time at home when the kids were growing up. I just realised, just recently, what a beautiful bunch of people they all turned out to be. I never knew how hard it was for you to grow them up. I wish I'd ... I'm sorry I didn't ... help you more.' (Eddie)
>
> 'Everyone up on Murray knows you're Benny's boy.' (Killoran)

Throughout *Mabo* we see Netta's steady and firm belief in the importance of raising her children and caring for her family. For Netta, this is the way they will survive. Eddie, towards the end of his life, also realises the value of this, tearfully thanking Netta for the family she has held together while he fought for the broader political rights of his family.

There are several scenes where we see that Eddie's family, as well as his ideological battles, is deeply important to him. A key example is at the Mabo dinner table, where we see the handing down of traditional cultural knowledge across barriers of blood and geography (Chapter Six). We have previously seen a flashback of Benny teaching his adopted son Eddie the laws of their island. Now we see Eddie show off, for Noel and Henry, the teachings he has instilled in his son – even though Eddie's children have all grown up far from the island where Malo's laws apply. As Eddie watches his son proudly, the scene is intercut with flashbacks of Benny teaching Eddie these same laws. This shows that the bonds of family can transcend distance and chronology, and reminds us of Eddie's belief in his heritage and, through his children, in his future.

Family as support

An idea underlying the narrative is that family connections can build an individual's identity and resilience. We see this in the strength of Eddie and Netta's family life, despite their conflicts, as well as in Eddie's connection to his own familial background. Interestingly, this background is not a biological one but a social and emotional one. Eddie considers Benny and Maiga Mabo his father and mother.

In Chapter Nine, Margaret White presents evidence to the court that Eddie has resisted his birth father and brother, instead maintaining the connection with the Mabos, his adopted family: '… you wished to be a Mabo … and you have always maintained this position'. Although she presents this with the aim of destabilising Eddie's hereditary claim to the land on Murray Island, her argument inadvertently illustrates and confirms the strength of Eddie's commitment to his adoptive family, ultimately devaluing the importance of a biological connection.

Similarly, Killoran, while trying to intimidate Eddie when they meet in a hallway during the court case, is forced to acknowledge Eddie's connection to the Mabos when he says, 'I know Benny Mabo raised you' (Chapter Nine). Although his ensuing comments are clearly hurtful, he only serves to strengthen Eddie's resolve and commitment to his heritage and land entitlements.

The text argues that individuals are strengthened by their connection to family – whether that connection is based in biology or arises from choice; whether it is with one's ancestors or with one's descendants.

Q Do you think Eddie's desire to be considered a Mabo is based on the power and cultural wealth this heritage entitles him to? What other reasons might he have for maintaining his identity as a Mabo?

Q Is there any evidence in the text to suggest that family connections make individuals vulnerable, instead of resilient?

DIFFERENT INTERPRETATIONS

Different interpretations arise from different responses to a text. Over time, a text will give rise to a wide range of responses from its audiences, who may come from various social or cultural groups and live in very different places and historical periods. Responses by critics and reviewers can be published in newspapers, journals and books, both online and in print. They can also be expressed in discussions that take place in the media, classrooms, book groups and so on.

While there is no single correct reading or interpretation of a text, it is important to understand that an interpretation is more than a personal opinion – it is the justification of a point of view on the text. To present an interpretation of a text based on your point of view, you must use a logical argument and support it with relevant evidence from the text.

Reception and reviews

Reviews following the ABC's first broadcast of Mabo on 10 June 2012 varied in their response and interpretation, although most were positive. Some of the critics' responses are summarised below (links to these reviews are provided in the 'References' section). It should be noted that with the exception of Graeme Blundell's review for *The Australian*, these reviews are brief and do not offer much specific support or evidence for their views. This is appropriate for their genre; this text was a telemovie for a popular audience, so the reviews are similarly 'popularist' in style, rather than in-depth critical, analytical or academic responses. Remember that when you discuss this text, however, you should support it in the same way you support your discussions of the other texts you study, using specific examples and details. (For more advice on discussing the text, see 'Questions and answers'.)

Ruth Ritchie's *Sydney Morning Herald* review is short and mostly complimentary, commending the production for bringing to national attention the life of a man who is important in our cultural history, but whose story is not widely known, compared to that of other Australians whose lives have already been the subject of biopics, such as Ita Buttrose. In fact, Ritchie highlights the distinction of *Mabo*'s central subject, and is tentative in her criticism of the production, even though it failed to completely satisfy her. For example, she cautiously suggests that Eddie's emotional motivations and experiences are at times inaccessible to the audience, but she softens this criticism by commending Deborah Mailman's performance as Netta, noting how she enhances the viewer's understanding of Eddie simply through her facial expressions. She also writes, however, that the love story is 'not always believable'.

In contrast, Katharine Rogers declares in her review for the website *Right Now* that 'the love story at the film's core, portrayed beautifully by the two leads, carries it through'. Similarly, Richard Watts, in his piece for *artsHub*, says of the love story that it is 'electric yet tender, and a key part of what makes this telemovie so successful'. While Rogers claims that the production has 'that "TV movie" feel to it' and 'is not particularly cinematic', Blundell compliments Rachel Perkins and her team on achieving their aims 'with bravura and a cinematic style that is often mesmerising'.

The contrasts between these opinions are a reminder of just how differently individuals can interpret the same text.

Blundell's review, which covers the production in more depth than the others mentioned here, offers detailed discussion of some of the cinematic aspects of *Mabo*, including the soundtrack, analysing how certain elements of the music function in the same way as elements of language function within a print text, contributing to the emotional and thematic development of the story.

Two interpretations

The following discussion demonstrates how two opposing interpretations of a text can both be supported with evidence from that text. Note that the two provide very different interpretations of character, but both are supported with specific examples of dialogue, behaviour or events.

Interpretation 1: *Mabo* is the story of a man whose pride and ambitions led him to act selfishly.

At the heart of *Mabo* is the story of Eddie Mabo, a man who had grand visions of his own importance, influence and value in the world. This can be seen in his actions, his relationships and others' perceptions of him. Although his legal battles achieved historic legislative change that improved the chances for many Indigenous people to gain legal recognition of their land rights, this utilitarian outcome (that is, an outcome that was practical and useful to many) was supplementary rather than central – merely a fortunate side effect of his own goals.

From Eddie's early days, we see his father, Benny Mabo, instilling in him a sense of confidence and entitlement. In flashbacks near the beginning of the telemovie, they walk along the beach on Murray Island, and Benny tells Eddie that his heritage is distinguished; he is descended from the 'clan of the holy ones'. Benny tells him, 'Everything here is yours. This is who you are.' Eddie, after his exile from the island, carries this belief through his adult life, even though he has not lived on the land or had a physical connection to it for many years.

As Margaret White, opposing counsel in Eddie's protracted land-rights claim against the Queensland government, puts it during case proceedings in the late 1980s: 'The problem is, is it not, Mr Mabo, that you haven't really resided in a meaningful way on Murray Island since 1956?' (Chapter Nine). The Murray Island Council reiterates this when Eddie nominates for membership – yet another instance of his inflated sense of his own importance. The council refuses his nomination because he hasn't lived there for nearly thirty years, and has in fact been 'troublemaking and agitating' on the mainland instead (Chapter Seven). Eddie counters with the fact that he plans to move back, 'when' (not if, but when) he wins the land-rights claim. He is arrogant enough not to even accept the possibility of losing, and he protests his own personal importance to the island, claiming his direct line of descent and connection to spiritual and cultural leaders of the land.

Others also perceive this sense of inflated importance, and it works against him during the court case. Margaret White quotes Eddie's original statement, which he claims not to recall, including declarations such as 'the council looks to me for social, political and legal advice. This is because of my hereditary title, which I alone can claim' and 'my arrival on the island rejuvenates hope among the people … I am the leader in the people's memory, according to tradition' (Chapter Nine). Although we know that he does have some hereditary right to land on Murray Island, his claims about his own reputation are clearly unsubstantiated. We have already seen how the Murray Island Council views him, and some of his fellow Islanders feel similarly, judging his land claim 'greedy' (Chapter Seven).

Eddie's delusions of grandeur reach almost megalomaniacal proportions in this scene, as he distorts his own importance to try to gain land. As the Minister for Aboriginal and Islander Affairs argues, it seems that Eddie is trying to 'own a very large proportion of Mer [Murray] Island and … use that as a springboard … for power'. The minister goes on to say Eddie is doing this at the expense of both the Australian taxpayers and those still living on the island (Chapter Seven). When this stage of the case concludes, this opinion is endorsed by Justice Moynihan, who finds in favour of the other plaintiffs but not Eddie, because he perceives him to be 'capable of tailoring his story to whatever shape he perceived would advance his cause' and too concerned with 'his own self-interest'.

The last area in which we see evidence of Eddie's selfishness is in the domestic realm. Time after time, Netta admonishes him for making decisions based on his activist goals, instead of caring for his growing family. Examples are when he quits his job (Chapter Four), and when he refuses to work, instead collecting unemployment benefits while he self-importantly takes the government to court. He later travels regularly, leaving Netta at home caring for the children as he flies across the country to meet lawyers, prioritising his own legal battles above the wellbeing of his family. When Netta finally snaps and refuses to listen to him discussing the case one evening – saying he's spoken of nothing else, while the children have survived 'on frozen fish and flour for nine years' – he responds to her with anger and intimations of violence, and threatens to treat the children the same way if it will get him 'a bit of respect'. After the argument he repents briefly and sources fish and vegetables for a cheerful family dinner, but this merely serves to highlight the family responsibilities he has neglected for so long.

Although he does finally advise his lawyers to take the case to the High Court for the sake of 'all the blackfellas' instead of appealing his own individual unsatisfactory result – an apparently unselfish decision – he still seeks his own glory. This is evidenced by the fact that he doesn't agree to the decision until his lawyer reassures him that he will still be publicly recognised: 'We're not taking your name off the case, Eddie' (Chapter Ten).

There is clear evidence, in both Eddie's own behaviour and others' perceptions of him, that he is a man whose sense of self-worth is disproportionate to the evidence. He believes in his own importance to the extent that he becomes selfish in his actions, such as those he takes in regard to the long-running land-rights case – a process for which he sacrifices his day-to-day family responsibilities.

Interpretation 2: *Mabo* is the story of a man who sacrificed everything for the good of his people.

Eddie Mabo was a man who fought tirelessly for the causes he believed in. *Mabo* celebrates his generosity of spirit in his commitment to improving the quality of life for his fellow Torres Strait Islanders and Indigenous people. The telemovie charts the progress of his ten-year legal battle, depicting how he sacrificed his own time, energy and material comfort to achieve historical results in the legal sphere of Australian race relations.

Eddie leaves his home on Murray Island as a young man, and lives for most of his life on mainland Australia. Yet he retains a spiritual, emotional and idealistic connection to his homeland – he reassures his mother, after marrying Netta, 'We'll be coming back for sure, Mum. For sure we'll be coming back' (Chapter Three). He also tells Henry Reynolds and Noel Loos, 'I've got this plan of one day going back up, setting up my shack up there … and live the old traditional way' (Chapter Six). His love for his island home is evident, even though his political passions keep him away for many years while he pursues the legal right to his hereditary land. Although he would like to be living on Murray Island, he chooses instead to fight for legal recognition that will pave the way for others to own their land too. He explains to the Murray Island Council that he will return to the island once he wins the land-rights claim, a case that is 'the most important thing that will happen to this island in two hundred years' (Chapter Seven). He stays away from his beloved home until he can change the non-Indigenous laws and perceptions that regulate the Islanders' lives.

Eddie's idealistic commitment to improving the lives of others has its roots early in his working life, when he becomes an active union member on the railway and at the waterfront, encouraging other Islander workers to join too, in order to agitate for better recognition, training and conditions. He eventually quits his job in order to fight for 'black causes', telling Netta that they should start housing co-ops, community schools and workers' unions; march for awareness and rights; and find ways to make things better for Indigenous people. When Netta asks him how they can do that, he says, 'Any way we can!' (Chapter Four). Clearly he is willing to make sacrifices for the greater good, and we see him follow through on these ideals, such as by running the community school.

Eddie wants to own his own land, but he is also committed to the broader cause: as he says to a fellow Islander, 'It's not about your land or my land ... It's about people' (Chapter Seven). His motivation for pursuing the land-rights claim for so many years – even when he has no money, and even when he is faced with challenges and failure, over and over – is not just for his own interest but, as with his union activity, to 'make things better' (Chapter Four) for others.

A key scene illustrating Eddie's unselfish commitment to his cause occurs in Chapter Ten, after a disappointing result in his land-rights claim. Eddie's lawyers advise him that his alternatives are to appeal the case or take the issue to the High Court. Eddie realises that he can continue to fight for his own land or sacrifice his individual case in the interests of the cause: 'If I appeal, it's about Eddie Mabo's land. If I don't, and then you take it to the High Court, it's about all the blackfellas, isn't it? ... Not just the Islanders – on the mainland, too.' After seeking brief clarification from his lawyer, his decision is made with barely any hesitation: 'Forget the appeal. Go to the High Court.'

The climax of the telemovie is the scene in Chapter Twelve when the High Court finally hands down its decision in Eddie's favour, overturning the notion of terra nullius in a historic move. Although the results of the case are significant and worthy of celebration, Eddie is not there to hear the decision, having died from cancer several months earlier. In this sad ending to the story, we see how Eddie symbolically sacrificed his whole life to the cause, having fought for so many years, and dying without ever receiving the glory, recognition or appreciation he deserved.

QUESTIONS & ANSWERS

This section focuses on your own analytical writing on the text, and gives you strategies for producing high-quality responses in your coursework and exam essays.

Essay writing – an overview

An essay on a text is a formal and serious piece of writing that presents your point of view on that text, usually in response to a given topic. Your 'point of view' in an essay is your interpretation of the meaning of the text's language, structure, characters, situations and events, supported by detailed analysis of textual evidence.

Analyse – don't summarise

In your essays it is important to avoid simply summarising what happens in a text.

- A **summary** is a description or paraphrase (retelling in different words) of the characters and events. For example: 'Macbeth has a horrifying vision of a dagger dripping with blood before he goes to murder King Duncan.'
- An **analysis** is an explanation of the real meaning or significance that lies 'beneath' the text's words (and images, for a film). For example: 'Macbeth's vision of a bloody dagger shows how deeply uneasy he is about the violent act he is contemplating – as well as his sense that supernatural forces are impelling him to act.'

A limited amount of summary is sometimes necessary to let your reader know which part of the text you wish to discuss. However, always keep this to a minimum and follow it immediately with your analysis of what this part of the text is really telling us.

Plan your essay

Carefully plan your essay so that you have a clear idea of what you are going to say. The plan ensures that your ideas flow logically, that your argument remains consistent and that you stay on the topic. An essay plan should be a list of **brief dot points** – no more than half a page.

- Include your central argument or main contention – a concise statement (usually in a single sentence) of your overall response to the topic. See 'Analysing a sample topic' for guidelines on how to formulate a main contention.
- Write three or four dot points for each paragraph indicating the main idea and evidence/examples from the text. Note that in your essay you will need to *expand* on these points and *analyse* the evidence.

Structure your essay

An essay is a complete, self-contained piece of writing. It has a clear beginning (the introduction), middle (several body paragraphs) and end (the last paragraph or conclusion). It must also have a central argument that runs throughout, linking each paragraph to form a coherent whole.

See examples of introductions and conclusions in the 'Analysing a sample topic' and 'Sample answer' sections.

The introduction establishes your overall response to the topic. It includes your main contention and outlines the main evidence you will refer to in the course of the essay. Write your introduction *after* you have done a plan and *before* you write the rest of the essay.

The body paragraphs argue your case – they present evidence from the text and explain how this evidence supports your argument. Each body paragraph needs:

- a strong **topic sentence** (usually the first sentence) that states the main point being made in the paragraph
- **evidence** from the text, including some brief quotations

- **analysis** of the textual evidence, explaining its significance, and **explanation** of how it supports your argument
- **links back to the topic** in one or more statements, usually towards the end of the paragraph.

Connect the body paragraphs so that your discussion flows smoothly. Use some linking words and phrases such as 'similarly' and 'on the other hand', though don't start every paragraph like this. Another strategy is to use a significant word from the last sentence of one paragraph in the first sentence of the next.

Use key terms from the topic – or synonyms for them – throughout, so the relevance of your discussion to the topic is always clear.

The conclusion ties everything together and finishes the essay. It includes strong statements that emphasise your central argument and provide a clear response to the topic.

Avoid simply restating the points made earlier in the essay – this will end on a very flat note and imply that you have run out of ideas and vocabulary. The conclusion is meant to be a logical extension of what you have written, not just a repetition or summary of it. Writing an effective conclusion can be a challenge. Try using these tips:

- Start by linking back to the final sentence of the second-last paragraph – this helps your writing to 'flow', rather than leaping back to your main contention straight away.
- Use synonyms and expressions with equivalent meanings to vary your vocabulary. This allows you to reinforce your line of argument without being repetitive.
- When planning your essay, think of one or two broad statements or observations about the text's wider meaning. These should be related to the topic and your overall argument. Keep them for the conclusion, since they will give you something 'new' to say but still follow logically from your discussion. The introduction will be focused on the topic, but the conclusion can present a wider view of the text.

Essay topics

1 'The use of cinematic techniques enhances the narrative in *Mabo*.' Discuss.

2 A placard in one of the archival protest scenes claims, "Unity is strength." How does *Mabo* illustrate the importance of unity?

3 '*Mabo* is as much a work of fiction as it is a story of the facts.' Discuss.

4 '*Mabo* focuses closely on Eddie; we are only interested in the other characters in terms of how they relate to Eddie's story.' Discuss.

5 Benny Mabo says to Eddie, "Young men go to the mainland … they forget everything." To what extent does Eddie's life reflect this statement?

6 'Because we do not see much of Eddie's early life, it is difficult for us to sympathise with his apparent connection to his homeland.' Discuss.

7 'Events are more important than characters in *Mabo*.' Do you agree?

8 'Eddie could not have succeeded without Netta.' Discuss.

9 "Koiki's the one." Is Eddie Mabo a hero?

10 Several scenes feature Eddie's sketches or paintings of his island home. How does *Mabo* illustrate the old adage, "Home is where the heart is"?

Vocabulary for writing on *Mabo*

Indigenous and non-Indigenous: When discussing issues in this telemovie such as Australian race relations, it is important to maintain an awareness of terminology. Eddie and fellow Islanders, for example, might use terms such as 'blackfella' to refer to themselves, or 'whitefella' to describe non-Indigenous characters, but these would not be appropriate terms to use in an academic discussion of the characters (unless directly quoting characters themselves). 'Indigenous' and 'non-Indigenous' are terms relatively free from controversy, and therefore are suitable to use in this situation.

Telemovie, text, narrative: Remember that the 'text' you are studying is in the form of a telemovie – similar to a television series or a film but with subtle differences (for example, in scope, length and production techniques). If you want to refer specifically to the events or details of the plot (rather than the way they are communicated to us), you might simply talk about the text or the narrative.

Analysing a sample topic

'The use of cinematic techniques enhances the narrative in *Mabo*.' Discuss.

A broad prompt like this invites you to consider how the construction of the text (in this case, the technical elements contributing to the narrative) impacts upon your understanding and appreciation of it. Here, significant factors to discuss might include genre, the meaning of the text and particular technical strategies.

Your first step should always be to ensure that you understand the key terms in a topic, whether these are words quoted from the text, technical terminology (such as 'cinematic' or 'narrative') or instructional/directional aspects of the topic (such as 'discuss'). A good way to do this is to jot down your initial understanding and then look up the words in a dictionary (using more than one dictionary can offer you more detail, and help ensure that you really understand the terms). Then write out your new understanding. You might also like to use brainstorming strategies to jot down any associations or specific examples that spring to mind in relation to your particular text.

Next, you will need to gather and organise evidence from the text in order to discuss the topic. Evidence frequently consists of quotations or events from a text, but in this case the focus is very specific: cinematic techniques. However, this does not mean that you can ignore all the other content of the text. Rather, you must draw links between this particular element and the rest of the telemovie, in order to analyse how the cinematic techniques contribute to the overall effectiveness of the text.

When you are clear about the meaning and requirements of the essay question, you will need to frame a contention. With this prompt, there are two basic options: you can agree or disagree with the statement. In this case, the instruction is to 'discuss'. This means you do not necessarily need to argue strongly for one side or the other: your contention may be that the cinematic techniques do contribute to the narrative, but that (as the review by Rogers suggests) the telemovie fails to make enough use of these techniques. Choosing to disagree (or partially disagree) with an essay prompt often leads you to a more interesting response, but it is also more challenging.

Below is a brief outline of how you might approach an answer that agrees with the prompt.

Sample introduction

> Television and cinema generally communicate narratives using language, just as novels or other written texts do. But the medium also offers the opportunity of enhancing the storyline with other layers of meaning constructed by elements such as cinematography, editing, lighting and sound. The docudrama *Mabo* employs many such techniques in order to facilitate and deepen our understanding of its events, characters and themes. In this way, the text is able to tell compellingly the story of Eddie Mabo's life: his activism and fights for Indigenous land rights, his connection to his traditional land on Murray Island and his love for his family – particularly his wife, Netta.

Body paragraph outline

Paragraphs 2–3: The scene in which Eddie receives his father's parcel demonstrates how various cinematic techniques enhance the narrative.

- When Eddie receives a parcel from his father – a coconut and a letter (the contents of which are conveyed in voice-over) – we see how he longs for his home, as the taste of the coconut and the words of his father conjure a flashback to the scene from the film's opening. This footage is in slow motion, contributing to the sense that it is an important moment in the text.
- The use of flashback offers us access to Eddie's internal thought processes and memories. It also adds a sense of melancholy to his memory of the past (when compared to his hot, dusty, lonely present), illustrating his homesickness.
- The use of voice-over allows us to experience both Benny's thoughts and Eddie's reaction simultaneously, reminding us of the importance of their relationship to each other.

Paragraphs 4–5: The wedding scene also demonstrates how various cinematic techniques enhance the narrative.

- When Eddie approaches Netta's cousin's wedding, hoping to speak with Netta, we know immediately that he is intoxicated. In the previous shot, he was sipping rum; when he approaches the wedding, although he walks steadily, the shot has a handheld-camera feel, the camera wavering from side to side and thus offering viewers an insight into Eddie's slightly wobbly state of mind.
- Combining dialogue and cinematic techniques strengthens our understanding: when Eddie drops the rum, he is accused of bringing in the 'devil's filth', the dialogue reiterating the drunkenness that we have inferred.
- The reaction shots that follow occur in slow motion, allowing us to watch Eddie and Netta's glances at each other, thus enhancing the narrative with non-verbal, emotional information about their experience.
- Editing decisions highlight contrast: the gentle pastels inside the hall contrast with the darkness outside, and a stabilised camera shot contrasts with previous (and subsequent) handheld-camera shots

following Eddie; this foreshadows later differences between Eddie and Netta.

Sample conclusion

While some of the narrative information in *Mabo* is conveyed through conventional textual techniques – such as through dialogue – much of the meaning is communicated, or at least strengthened, by other cinematic techniques, including editing decisions, camera movement, film speed, lighting and colour. These offer information beyond the verbal, and in doing so allow us access to characters' subjective emotional experiences. These techniques also contribute symbolic meaning to the narrative; for example, when Eddie and Netta first meet the film's visual language conveys a distinct contrast between their experiences, anticipating some of the conflicts that will later emerge as a result of their differing approaches to life. In many ways, then, *Mabo*'s use of cinematic techniques enriches our understanding of the narrative.

SAMPLE ANSWER

A placard in one of the archival protest scenes claims, "Unity is strength." How does *Mabo* illustrate the importance of unity?

Although *Mabo* is the story of one man's life, and particularly of his passion and dedication to the legal battle for ownership of his land, it also shows us that Eddie Mabo could never have achieved the watershed result he did without the knowledge, comradeship, support and love of others. From Eddie's early union activism, through his long court case, to his enduring relationship with his wife, Netta, we see how both his individual resilience and his connection to those around him offer the strength necessary to succeed in the challenges he faces.

The word 'unity', interestingly, can convey two quite different meanings. One is the idea of being a single entity, complete and autonomous; the other is almost the opposite: the notion of agreement, commonality, and shared values and goals among two or more people. It is this second meaning that the placard in the protest is referring to, as the protester advocates for the importance of shared goals, and the impact of many voices, rather than just one. In political activism, the fight for rights, recognition and change can only be undertaken when many stand together as one – when unity provides strength.

In *Mabo*, the importance of this second meaning of unity is primarily what is illustrated. However, Eddie's individual strength of character is also celebrated, as he maintains his integrity in his beliefs, values and love throughout his life, and these things are ultimately at the core of his remarkable legal triumphs. While Eddie is strong in himself, he only succeeds in his challenges because he recognises the value of the second meaning of unity. This is demonstrated throughout *Mabo* in the relationships he maintains with his colleagues; his lawyers; his friends; and his wife, Netta. Each of these relationships is an example of unity, and each offers strength to Eddie.

Eddie's early union activism is a perfect illustration of the slogan 'unity is strength'. The essence of unionism is that by sharing goals, values and approaches, individual workers can find strength, support and protection. By joining the union, Eddie is able to combine forces with his fellow Indigenous workers, strengthening both his and their positions in the workforce. He writes home to his father, explaining that he's been signing up the Islander rail workers to the union to 'make sure that we get a fair go'. Later in Eddie's working life, we see him planning to start a union for waterfront workers in order to offer strength to his colleagues.

Socially, too, unity with others brings strength. This is exemplified in Eddie's friendship with Noel Loos and Henry Reynolds. The three men share beliefs (as Noel observes during his first meeting with Eddie) and values, and they are able to offer support to one another along the difficult 'road of the activist'. This support is partly moral and partly in the form of information: they share experiences and knowledge in order to expand one another's education and understanding of the Indigenous rights issues they all hope to pursue. Their unity is mutually beneficial, as their connection strengthens each of them individually.

With this strength and support, Eddie begins to pursue his historic land-rights claim after attending a talk with Henry and Noel, where they meet Greg McIntyre and Barbara Hocking, who share Eddie's convictions and beliefs and are just waiting for a plaintiff to attempt a land-rights claim. Together, Eddie and these lawyers share a unity that strengthens their approach to the legal case – neither party would have been able to mount the case without the other.

There is further unity strengthening this case: the support from fellow Islanders Dave and Sam Passi and James Rice. As with union activism, the more voices there are, the stronger their ability to fight. When Barbara Hocking says they will need a plaintiff, Eddie and Dave show their unity when they offer themselves, and Eddie says 'all of us' – gesturing to his fellow Islanders beside him, but symbolically suggesting a much broader unity, formed of his whole family and community. Later, when Dave Passi re-joins the case (after withdrawing in response to intimidation), we see Eddie and his lawyers' gratitude and joy at his return: there is strength in numbers, and such unity will bring this much-needed strength to the case.

The last and very significant illustration of the strength offered by unity is the relationship between Netta and Eddie. Netta's support for Eddie is, as he acknowledges in his final voice-over, what has helped him through the long legal claims – 'over many hardships and hurdles … somehow we made it'. We have seen them face the world as a solid unit, sharing love, values and commitments, such as when they run the school together, raise their family together, and, ultimately, fight the legal battle together. Eddie's last appearance in court reiterates this unity: as the High Court lawyers enter and the final iteration of the case begins, Netta clasps Eddie's hand, an image which is a strong symbol of the strength in unity.

In all areas of Eddie's life, then, we see how his existing strength is augmented by the strength found by sharing values and goals with colleagues, peers, community and family. The placard proclaiming 'unity is strength' is displayed in the specific context of an activist protest for Indigenous rights, but the concept is applicable to many other contexts, as *Mabo* illustrates.

REFERENCES & READING

Text

Mabo 2012, dir. Rachel Perkins, Blackfella Films. Starring Jimi Bani and Deborah Mailman.

References

Books

Broome, Richard 2009, *Aboriginal Australians: A History Since 1788*, 4th revised edition, Allen and Unwin, Sydney.

Loos, Noel and Mabo, Koiki 1996, *Edward Koiki Mabo: His Life and Struggle for Land Rights*, University of Queensland Press, Brisbane.

Covers much of Eddie's story in his own words, plus Noel's writings about his long friendship with Eddie.

Reynolds, Henry 2000, *Why Weren't We Told? A Personal Search for the Truth About our History*, Melbourne University Publishing, Melbourne.

Newspaper and journal articles

Blundell, Graeme 2012, 'Mabo Adheres to the First Principles of Biography', *The Australian*, 9 June, http://www.theaustralian.com.au/arts/review/first-principles/story-fn9n8gph-1226386585410#

Ritchie, Ruth 2012, 'Law of the Land', *Sydney Morning Herald*, 9 June, http://www.smh.com.au/entertainment/tv-and-radio/law-of-the-land-20120607-1zx6n.html

Rogers, Katharine 2012, 'Sydney Film Festival Review – Mabo', in *Right Now: Human Rights in Australia*, 9 June, http://rightnow.org.au/artwork/sydney-film-festival-review-%E2%80%93-mabo

Transcripts

Keating, Paul 1993, 'Opportunity and Care, Dignity and Hope', National Archives of Australia, www.primeministers.naa.gov.au/galleries/audio/transcript-m3983-749.aspx

Websites

Mabo 2012, ABC Television, www.abc.net.au/tv/mabo

Contains production background, in addition to useful resources such as interviews about the production of the telemovie, video documentaries relating to Eddie Mabo and the case, and further resources regarding native title. There is also a timeline incorporating videos and information – a particularly interesting item is located at 1988 on the timeline: an archival Radio National Law Report story giving detailed background on Eddie Mabo's claims, and including some interviews with Eddie.

Torres Strait Island Regional Council 2013, 'Mer (Murray Island)', www.tsirc.qld.gov.au/Mer

Watts, Richard 2012, 'Mabo', *artsHub*, 5 June, http://www.artshub.com.au/news-article/reviews/film-radio-tv/mabo-189729

Information about Murray and neighbouring islands, as well as links to broader information about the Torres Strait region.

Wellington, Rob, *Mabo – The Native Title Revolution*, Screen Australia Digital Learning, www.mabonativetitle.com

An extensive website based on an educational CD-ROM. Offers detailed history about the Mabo land claim, several documentary films, and other resources such as a copy of the land claim document.